STEAL THESE IDEAS!

SECOND EDITION

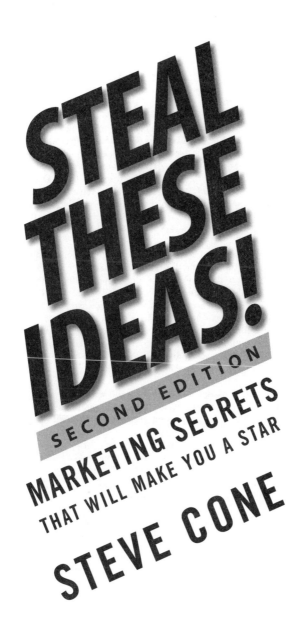

STEAL THESE IDEAS!

SECOND EDITION

MARKETING SECRETS
THAT WILL MAKE YOU A STAR

STEVE CONE

BLOOMBERG PRESS
An Imprint of

WILEY

Published by John Wiley & Sons, Inc., Hoboken, New Jersey.
Published simultaneously in Canada.

For general information on our other products and services or for technical support, please contact our Customer Care Department within the United States at (800) 762–2974, outside the United States at (317) 572–3993 or fax (317) 572–4002.

Wiley also publishes its books in a variety of electronic formats. Some content that appears in print may not be available in electronic books. For more information about Wiley products, visit our web site at www.wiley.com.

Library of Congress Cataloging-in-Publication Data:
Cone, Steve, 1950-
    Steal these ideas!: marketing secrets that will make you a star / Steve Cone.—2nd ed.
        p.   cm.— (Bloomberg; 144)
    Includes index.
    ISBN 978–1–118–00444–9 (cloth); ISBN 978-0-470-88304-4 (ebk);
    ISBN 978-0-470-88382-2 (ebk); ISBN 978-0-470-88507-9 (ebk)
    1. Marketing. I. Title.
HF5415.C54738 2011
658.8—dc23
                                                            2011021458

Printed in the United States of America
10 9 8 7 6 5 4 3 2 1

To Cliff
Father and Son. Pals Forever.

CONTENTS

INTRODUCTION

"**W**hat do we do now?"

This question is reverberating throughout the land in businesses large and small as America and the overall global economy sit mired in a protracted weak economic recovery as the "Great Recession" recedes ever so slowly. But before you reach for your fourth scotch of the night or plug in a Valium drip, why not relax a bit and get ready to focus. Focus on the few simple but powerful marketing techniques that never change regardless of the ever-changing marketing landscape and the digital world that envelops us today.

This second edition of *Steal These Ideas!* can help any size business not only stay in business but even prosper as the competition falters and in some cases fail.

Indeed, there is nothing like seemingly endless drab economic conditions for businesses to hone in on what really drives sales and a growing bottom line. You can forget all the theory, all the pie charts, all the organizational consultants, and, yes, the vast majority of those who teach marketing in universities and business schools. What you should remember are four simple Steve Cone marketing maxims:

1. Your brand is a promise that delivers an experience—hopefully, a unique and value-added one.
2. Marlboro has been the leading cigarette brand by far since 1955, and you don't have to sell a politically incorrect product to achieve this type of success.

3. Do the reverse of whatever GM does.

4. Social networking started 10,000 years ago. We can learn a lot from its humble beginnings.

I will elaborate on these four points throughout the chapters that make up this new edition.

Phil Kotler, one of the best-known marketing professors of all time once proclaimed, "Marketing takes a day to learn but a lifetime to master." I disagree that successful marketing outcomes must take many years to perfect, because what makes a company grow, even in extremely difficult economic times, is a realization that job one and two and three is to ramp up direct communication with your very best customers or potential customers and get them to brag to friends and family and even strangers about why your company stands out from the pack and deserves their business now and in the future.

I have good news. Unlike other eras of slow-growth economies like the early 1980s, marketers today have the database and communication tools to *wow* customers and qualified prospects in a highly efficient and cost-effective manner.

And, ironically, a world-class example of the power of digital-age marketing comes not from the commercial sector but from the political world. While other candidates in the last presidential election fumbled and bumbled around, the Obama team used simple-to-understand techniques to outmarket the competition. I will give concrete examples of how to follow this same path for your product or service. And I will do more than that—I will also show what type of promotions to totally avoid and why. And more than that—the simple techniques that can be slam-dunks for your business in the digital age or any age.

Like my first book, this one is a quick read. It gives you a lot of new material not covered or only briefly mentioned in the first edition. Also, you will again be able to see a marked improvement in your company's sales almost immediately by following my advice and guidance. Very few of the ideas revealed are purely original thinking—after all, who wants that? What you want and will get is advice that has been proven to work over and over again and yet today is not widely understood or practiced.

Fundamentally, you will learn how simple and straightforward it is to create promotions with immediate and lasting impact that increase sales and enhance customer loyalty in the process. All of the techniques you can "steal" in the chapters to follow are straightforward and for the most part right out of that Psychology 101 class you snored through your freshman year in college.

But now it is time to *wake up*. In fact, it's past time.

Steve Cone
New York City
June 2011

CHAPTER 1

BILLIONS AND BILLIONS WASTED...

I have the opportunity a few times a year to be a guest speaker at chamber of commerce events across America where local business owners pay a few bucks to enjoy a decent lunch or dinner and listen to me telling them that the size of a business has zero correlation to marketing prowess. In fact, most of the multinational world-class brands waste billions of dollars every year trying to establish a permanent beachhead in consumers' minds with brand promises (taglines) that gain no traction and no home in a single memory cell among the billions that we each possess.

If you don't believe me—and without googling—ask yourself what are Coke's or Pepsi's current taglines. You have no clue despite the zillions of impressions they keep shelling out online and offline every minute of every day. These are pure marketing-driven companies with huge ad budgets that also happen to be mortal business enemies. You would think one of the two would have enough collective marketing brainpower to understand how to create a brand promise that gets consumers to pay attention instead of doing the opposite.

You would assume either of these companies could create just the right few words to provide a memorable tagline that consumers would enjoy and remember as they did decades ago when Coke and Pepsi knew what they were doing. And you would be totally wrong. My speaking tour confirms that what consumers of all ages remember if asked to recall a Coke or Pepsi tagline are a Coke line from the 1940s and again used in the 1970s and a Pepsi line from the 1960s. For Coke: "It's the real thing." For Pepsi: "You're in the Pepsi generation." It's amazing that no one has a clue what their current taglines are. Which just goes to prove what I have been saying for years to companies I consult with: *never change a great line.*

One major reason memorable and effective taglines get discarded is that company brass think consumers get bored with "the same old line." As I will prove again and again throughout this book, the only folks who get bored are the company's senior managers. Most of us make the huge mistake of thinking consumers are just like us. We think about our company constantly, often day and night, weekends and holidays, and never really take a mental break from our management chores. Our customers, however, only think about us every so often when they have a specific need we can meet or they happen to notice an ad or open a promotional letter or catalog. The point is that they rarely concern themselves with our brand. And when they do, they don't

---

Never Change a Great Line—The Proof: BMW

The facts speak for themselves. Over the past 45 years the one auto manufacturer with the best profitability record is BMW. And BMW is the only company in the industry that has kept the same tagline/brand promise for almost a half century—"The ultimate driving machine." In recall test after test, this is the only auto tagline that is immediately remembered by consumers. There is no mystery to this recall; the real mystery is why BMW's competitors do not understand the power of keeping the same brand promise and thus staying top-of-mind in the category literally forever—talk about ultimate marketing.

want to be confused. They want to know that the company they buy from stands for what it has always stood for. That is why I repeat: *never change a great line.*

Oh, the other reason great taglines get discarded is a new chief marketing officer (CMO) wants to prove his worth and launch a new brand promise—beyond stupid, and if you are the chief executive officer (CEO), never allow that to happen.

McDonald's Almost Gets It

The theme of this chapter is billions of dollars wasted on dead-on-arrival brand promises/taglines—and by companies that should know better. A company with billions of product served since its founding (which should know better) is McDonald's. Just like at McDonald's, where billions of burgers have landed in the stomachs of millions of consumers worldwide, billions and billions of impressions assault our brains during our lifetime. What we remember and what we forget is what marketers constantly strive to figure out so their product/service messages wind up in the remembered part of our cortex. The approach most marketers take is to "keep up with the times" and change their brand promise or tagline on a regular basis. (Coke has used over 90 taglines in their 120-year history, or as I like to say—they have used 88 too many). Nothing could be dumber. McDonald's doesn't get it all wrong. They have kept their core customer proposition, which for them is two words generally seen on the large outdoor McDonald's sign at each establishment: "Billions Served."

In a sense, "Billions Served" is McDonald's motto—a statement of fact and a guiding principle of the franchise. They have gone beyond just having a motto since the 1960s by creating new taglines every few years such as their current line: "I'm lovin' it." Is this "replace the tagline every so often" a good idea? No.

We can travel all the way back to the last few centuries of the Roman Empire to see that sometimes a single well-chosen word is enough to last for the ages.

Consider the word *sincerely*, which I mentioned briefly in the first edition of this book. It originated around 50 AD from the Latin *in sine cere*, which means "without wax." During that period, many Roman marble merchants were lax with their wax and went about selling marble as perfect, when they knew the opposite to be true. They would sell cracked marble as void of imperfections by filling in the cracks with wax. Buyers were not amused when after the sale they discovered the ruse. It got so bad the Roman government stepped in and issued an edict that pure marble for sale had to be labeled *sine cere*, meaning there was no wax filling in any cracks. The penalty for ignoring this early brand promise was death to the merchant. We have been using *sincerely* ever since, though not at fear for our lives.

A 20th-century example of one word commanding great respect and burned in our collective memory came from Franklin Roosevelt's declaration of war on Japan on December 8, 1941. His speech was originally going to begin: "December 7, 1941, a day that will live in world history. . . ." Then, at the last minute before going on live radio to the nation and the world, FDR scribbled out world history and wrote in the word *infamy*. This change transformed an ordinary sentence into an extraordinary one that will be remembered for all time.

In the first decade of the 21st century, we have all but forgotten how powerful a few well-chosen words can be and how critical for businesses of any size to have a chance at breaking through promotional clutter amounting in U.S. dollars to $60 billion monthly spent worldwide on advertising and related activities.

Few companies today have a clue about how to create and maintain a brand promise with just the right words to propel them to the top of their category and then stay at the top indefinitely.

New Challenges We Face and Five Rules to Live By

Several trends have emerged that are radically changing the way we interact with one another and are making the job of successfully promoting one's company ever harder by the minute. Three of these trends are:

1. The more we use the Internet, the more advertising loses the emotional appeal it needs to close a sale (the net effect of a small screen and often poor sound quality).
2. The breakup of the traditional family unit means millions of people crave one-on-one companionship and seek it through using digital dating services that provide an endless stream of possible matchups.
3. Belonging to something with potential celebrity status, no matter how fleeting, has never been more important and sought after. Think of the millions of participants on Facebook and Twitter as two examples. Plus, there is the attraction of such shows as *American Idol,* which is routinely the top-rated TV program in America.

What these trends tell us is that consumers moving at digital speed to communicate with each other do not have the time or the interest in having brands they have come to rely on keep changing their brand promise. Additionally, it has never been more important to create an emotional connection through a unique way of describing your offering that appeals to consumers who are otherwise bombarded with endless streams of text, e-mail, mobile, and other messaging that delivers information but little if any personality.

Widely forgotten are a few simple rules (five) that can help you create a powerful tagline that can serve as your singular brand promise and launching pad for top-of-mind consumer awareness. And looking out through the next decade ahead, I see no change to these rules other than it will be even more critical to follow them as closely as possible.

Rule 1: Creating a Tagline Is an Art, Not a Science

Take your pick: "You deserve a break today" (McDonald's); "the ultimate driving machine" (BMW); "M'm m'm good" (Campbell Soup); "come to Marlboro country" (Marlboro cigarettes); "when you care enough to send the very best" (Hallmark); "it takes a tough man to make a tender chicken" (Purdue); "The few. The proud. The Marines" (Marine Corps). These memorable lines and many more throughout the past 100 years were created by individual writers on assignment to pen just the right combination of words for a product or service to rise above and beyond the competition.

Companies today have no clue, and instead of hiring a gifted wordsmith, they engage at great expense in endless committee brainstorming (a total oxymoron) and consumer focus groups, which result in committee-created taglines—all "dead on arrival." These lines are unfocused and so general in meaning they could apply to any business and thus to none specifically. A few examples launched recently (company names excluded): "reach higher"; "moving ahead"; "the power of possibilities"; "the power to be better"; "the power of you"; "High performance. Delivered"; "your world delivered"; "this is what we do"; "the future is yours."

Amazing how low the bar has fallen. You can avoid the platitude trap by hiring a talented writer and allowing him to give you his best effort. Your job is to provide him with a concise description of the three core benefits or features of your company, product, or service.

Rule 2: Your Company Is Different—Say So

Every company has a distinct selling proposition waiting to be brought to light. Think of your business as a personality. What is it that is special, genuine, timeless, and even fun and wildly different? Then just say it or get a great writer to. Also use word play when possible. A few examples I particularly like that cross the spectrum of groups large to small are: Hebrew National Hotdogs, "we answer to a higher authority"; Compari, "the first time is never the best"; Gonzer Electrical Contractors, "let us check your shorts"; Volkswagen UK, "relieves gas pains"; Fresh Direct Food Delivery, "Our food is fresh. Our customers are spoiled"; the town of Summit, New Jersey, "Summit. Everything else is downhill."

Rule 3: We Buy from People or Characters Who Entertain Us

Humans are most fascinated with each other—a good thing for the continuation of the species. We look for guidance to religious leaders and have great interest, often too much, in celebrities. We pay rapt attention to political front runners, business icons, sports figures, particularly nasty swindlers and criminals, media spokespeople, and occasionally even authors.

Personality is all-consuming; while asleep, we even dream about people real and imagined. It is therefore quite perplexing that marketers think they can sell without the aid of a spokesperson or endearing human-like character. Is it essential? I believe it is because it dramatically boosts your chances of gaining consumer attention over your competition. The one caveat is that you must select a spokesperson or character that fits your selling premise and does not appear false or forced. Major past successes include Mr. Whipple, Karl Malden for American Express, Morris the Cat, Charlie Tuna, Ronald McDonald, Frank Purdue, the Jolly Green Giant, and the Pillsbury Doughboy. (More on this topic in a later chapter).

Rule 4: Sound Becomes Memory Like No Other Sense

Through hundreds of millions of years of evolution the animal and human mind is wired to accept and remember sound much more so than the other dominant sense, sight. If you have any doubt, think of your all-time favorite movie and then think of watching it without sound. It would have no impact at all. Although smell, taste, and touch are powerful, they are not part of the media mix from TV to radio to Internet and are of limited use in print. Taglines become firmly embedded in our memories if they are delivered with a unique sound signature—a special rhythm and inflection that has never been used before. Radio actually trumps TV in remembering sound because there are no visual distractions. The Internet is sound challenged a bit for two reasons: (1) the sound is often hard to hear, and (2) the screen of a computer or handheld device is too small to give the impact of a large TV screen.

Bottom line—make sure your tagline is spoken at every opportunity and with a unique inflection. Without a special sound signature, your chances of successful top-of-mind awareness decrease dramatically.

Rule 5: Never, Ever Change a Great Tagline

Companies continue to change their taglines at great expense and to no effect, from American Express to Coke to McDonald's, Federal Express, GE, and Ford, to name a few. What consumers remember are taglines each of these global brands used decades ago. Every new line they have tried since has achieved near zero recognition despite billions spent on launching them. I bet not a single reader knows what Coke's new tagline is that launched with great hype on the 2010 Super Bowl or, for that matter, Pepsi's on the same Super Bowl. It is shocking that these rivals for world cola domination who are marketing driven to the nth degree have no ability today to deliver a tagline that will be as iconic as the brand itself.

Coke should have never given up "It's the real thing." And Pepsi should have kept for all time "You're in the Pepsi generation."

Taglines that are distinctive, spot-on genuine, and compelling are timeless. They do not need tinkering or refreshing. What should be updated are the promotions done year after year that the tagline is headlining. That is the secret formula to effective marketing.

What about Political Slogans?

The word *slogan* comes from the Scottish Gaelic word *sluagh-ghairm,* pronounced "slogorm," and means "battle cry." How appropriate for politics!

As I state in my book *Powerlines,* there hasn't been a decent presidential campaign slogan since Ronald Reagan's campaigns in 1980 and 1984. John McCain's approach was a total disaster, with his team using over seven different slogans, which confused everyone and left the impression he was not an effective leader—hmm. . . .

It should not be that hard to create a powerful campaign slogan, and, as history shows, the right slogan can do a lot to help ensure a victory. Slogans work in one of two ways only: (1) they focus on a singular issue that Americans can rally around, or (2) they positively reinforce the personality of the candidate in a way that has tremendous appeal. Reagan used both approaches. In 1980, against Jimmy Carter he rode to victory using the theme: "Are you better off than you were four years ago?" Carter had presided over a horrible recession, and clearly the voters agreed that they were not better off. Then, in 1984, against Fritz Mondale the Reagan team focused on how better off Americans were after Reagan's first term with the slogan: "It's morning again in America." This slogan was the focal point and major theme of every campaign speech, every TV ad, and every press release, and perfectly reflected Reagan's eternal optimism about life in general and the future of America under his leadership for four more years.

Reagan beat Mondale with the greatest electoral landslide in American history. Mondale just barely (by 3,000 votes) won his home state of Minnesota.

Remember

About 98 percent of all taglines today have no staying power and are a complete and utter waste of money. They have no personality or attitude and no unique claim or promise. Many are created by committee—always a dead-wrong approach. Powerful taglines define brands for all time and are immune to changes in technology and the basic living patterns of present and future generations. "A diamond is forever" (written by a 27-year-old copywriter in 1948) will always define that gem as long as people inhabit Mother Earth. Taglines like this one are inspiring phrases created by gifted writers who see a clear and compelling brand promise and make it come to life to inspire, entertain, and enlighten the rest of us.

2

THREE HIDDEN INGREDIENTS IN EVERY WINNING PROMOTIONAL CAMPAIGN

No matter how large or small your business, your promotional efforts represent hard-won dollars that must be used effectively. Competitive pressure to create a standout winning strategy can be enormous. The bad news is that you can't play it safe and get any traction in today's marketplace. The good news is that you can minimize the risk and dramatically increase your chance of hitting the jackpot by following this simple rule: A successful promotional campaign must have three essential ingredients:

1. Excitement.
2. News.
3. A compelling call to action.

These three elements never change no matter how much the marketing landscape does, as technology drives new ways for consumers to interact with each other and the companies they buy from.

We are busier than ever with little time to spare. We're working harder and we're tired from multitasking that wasn't even a concept just a decade ago. We are focused on the minute-to-minute. We are dealing nonstop all day long with logistics and noise and traffic. It takes a carefully crafted campaign to make us pay attention to one marketing message versus thousands of others that assault us in the car, on the bus, while watching TV, shopping, surfing the Web, texting, e-mailing, and skimming a magazine and listening to the radio.

When selling anything to anybody, anywhere in the world, always ask yourself, "Does my ad, brochure, billboard, window display, radio spot, or Web home page create excitement, generate real news, and provide a reason to *stop* everything right now and order my product or service?"

Fundamentally, the job of the marketing professional is to excite the potential buyers, to get them to pay attention to his product or service message and not the other guy's. Most marketing campaigns fail badly in the excitement category and do even worse in creating a compelling call to action.

The whole point of any promotion is to be *noticed* and get a *response*. Marketing expenditures exceed $40 billion a month attempting to grab consumer attention, just in the United States.

Will anyone really pay attention to one more burger ad, one more beautiful older-looking couple seeking financial security by walking hand in hand on a deserted beach, one more gleaming auto isolated on a rain-slicked winding road in Monument Valley?

Take a look at the following stellar campaigns, all of which demonstrate the power of integrated marketing excitement, news value, and compelling calls to action.

The Ultimate Help-Wanted Ad

If pressed to pick my all-time favorite ad, it would be one placed by Sir Ernest Shackleton, the famous early-20th-century polar explorer. In 1913, Shackleton placed a very brief announcement in several London newspapers for volunteers for his upcoming South Pole expedition. He hoped to attract 50 to 75 inquiries. Five thousand hearty souls responded to:

> MEN WANTED for Hazardous Journey. Small wages, bitter cold, long months of complete darkness, constant danger, safe return doubtful. Honor and recognition in case of success.
>
> —Sir Ernest Shackleton

All three elements for promotional success: excitement, news, and a compelling call to action were wrapped up in just 26 words. No need to add a single syllable.

The Early Days of *Playboy* Magazine

In the early 1950s, when I was five or six, my dad was what we call today a "Mad Man" in reference to the popular TV series *Mad Men*. He was pretty vague about what he did at work all day and, as it turned out, with good reason. He was writing some of the very first promotional direct-mail letters for Hugh Hefner's then new and struggling publication, *Playboy* magazine.

These letters would be sent to compiled lists of men who subscribed to other men's magazines—which, of course, made sense. What was different was how my dad wrote these letters. He came up with the idea of writing them from the perspective of a *Playboy* Bunny. Each mailing included a picture of her in full Bunny regalia. The picture appeared on the letter, the reply device, and throughout the accompanying brochure, which included shots of her other Bunny pals. She even signed her name.

Consequently, millions of American men received letters in the mail from a "real live *Playboy* Bunny," describing the scintillating attributes of *Playboy* magazine: great fiction, social commentary, and, of course, more revealing pictures of her and her friends. This approach was dramatically more successful than Hefner's earlier attempts with the sub-scription offer coming from him as editor-in-chief—because it was just much more *exciting!*

Rolling Stone Magazine

Back in the 1970s, the notorious antiestablishment, self-proclaimed gonzo journalist Hunter S. Thompson was a managing editor of *Rolling Stone.* He authored a subscrip-tion renewal letter that was completely different from what any other magazine had ever contemplated.

The letter, short and to the point, declared that *Rolling Stone* was Thompson's only legitimate source of income. It went on to say that if you didn't respond, he would be thrown into utter despair and probably wind up in Needles, California, "sucking from a nitric oxide tank down to the bottom death blast of freon, listening to German tourists describe their coyote sightings."

Basically, Thompson threatened the recipient, demand-ing a response, or else. To underline the warning, the out-side envelope featured "I KNOW WHERE YOU LIVE" scrawled in large handwriting across the front. Not your everyday *Time* or *Newsweek* renewal letter, to be sure.

This direct-mail subscription effort was a huge success, and *Rolling Stone* used it the entire time Thompson was on the payroll. It was so much fun to read. So different. So Hunter Thompson. So exciting.

Pan American WorldPass and How Last Became First

By the time the late 1970s rolled around, the experience of fly-ing had been downgraded from glamorous and elite to mun-dane, overcrowded, and as torturous as a never-ending bus trip. Yet flights were full of corporate executives and middle managers winging their way across the country and around the world on a regular basis. Working hard, making money, getting ahead, these were not happy travelers.

Although the airlines reveled in their popularity, they were also aware of the growing dissatisfaction of their large bloc of business travelers. In a classic marketing moment, several major airlines decided that their best customers deserved to be singled out and rewarded for frequent travel. Thus, the frequent flyer programs were born.

These programs were really exciting for participants. At last, the airlines made a distinction between the tourist and the trooper. Flying for free and upgrading to first class were the big come-ons, and frequent flyers went to great lengths to make sure they stayed abreast of every new perk and bonus mile route. It is important to understand what a big deal the frequent flyer programs were at that time.

Working with a small team at Epsilon, I helped United Airlines create Mileage Plus, one of the first of these reward scenarios. Several years later, I was fortunate enough to create the last entry of a major airline into this new game: Pan American Airways' WorldPass, the richest of all the frequent flyer programs.

According to airline industry analysts, WorldPass probably contributed to Pan Am's ability to remain in business for an additional decade. This is a story about creating excitement and news value even when you are *the absolute last* business in your sector to recognize your top clients.

By 1981, all other major U.S. carriers had well-developed frequent flyer programs, and Pan Am was seeing the negative effect on their bottom line. So what to do? The company was lucky to have a marketing director at the time, Adam Aron, who had natural marketing instincts, flair, and an appreciation of the power of big ideas.

The typical frequent flyer marketing approach was not as generous as it appeared. At that time, the goal was to spend as little as possible to communicate with your business travelers, and to be as restrictive as possible in giving out award travel for miles earned.

Adam had a different idea. His charge to me was to create the most expensive-looking program with the richest award structure. He wanted to leapfrog the competition—all of which had well-established programs and, in most cases, a four- to five-year head start. Since Pan Am was the last to arrive at the dance, Adam was determined his airline would be the dress that everyone noticed.

This core promise of Pan Am's program was to reward individuals who flew a specific number of miles on an annual basis with a "world pass." This pass was an actual gold-colored plastic card that entitled you and a companion to fly anywhere on Pan Am's extensive worldwide system, first class, free for 30 days.

This strategy was a winner from day one. No other airline even remotely had such an award, nor could any of them match the worldwide route structure that Pan Am was famous for. The effect was immediate. WorldPass electrified passengers, Pan Am employees, and the trade press. Adam's focus on giving the customer something that was truly exciting and "richer" than the competition turned the whole industry inside out and left them scrambling to catch up.

So last-in became first in frequent flyers' minds. The initial direct-mail enrollment package sent to 80,000 frequent flyers contained a free round-trip domestic ticket good at any time within the next six months—no blackout dates, no ifs, ands, or buts other than the requirement to enroll in WorldPass. Response rates to this one letter were more than 50 percent. Probably an all-time high in direct-mail history, with the exception of responses to letters from the IRS!

Other Quick Airline Stories about Creating Customer Excitement

American Airlines—When you joined the Admirals Club in the early 1970s, you received an oversized certificate done in calligraphy and beautifully framed, asserting your club membership. These were hung in offices with pride and were real status symbols.

Continental Airlines—In the 1960s and 1970s, the legendary chairman, Robert Six, wrote a letter to the airline's best customers once or twice a year, a letter that often went on for pages. It was so personal, so beautifully written, so candid, that customers not only saved these letters as keepsakes but they also continued to fly Continental just to stay on the VIP mailing list.

Braniff International—In the late 1960s and throughout the 1970s, Braniff attracted attention with brightly colored planes, leather seats in all classes, fine dining on bone china, and flight attendants dressed in fashionable Halston outfits. People actually looked forward to boarding a Braniff plane—hard to image in this day and age.

One for the Gipper

In 1983, the Republican Senatorial Committee wanted to end the year with a big fund-raising push to their top 200,000 contributors. At the time, they regularly spent 50 cents apiece on highly personalized computer letters to their donor base.

Given their desire to top previous fund-raising efforts, I convinced them to try something totally different for the year-end appeal: a single but very special letter that would cost roughly $7 in the mail. They agreed, and the end result was a one-letter appeal that raised more net dollars (over $2 million) than their archrival, the Democratic Senatorial Committee, raised in an entire year.

Here's what went into that $7 letter:

- A mailing envelope made to look like a FedEx overnight package but actually sent express mail via the U.S. Postal Service.
- A two-page fund-raising letter with an embossed gold senatorial seal.
- An 8″ × 10″ four-color signed photograph of President Ronald Reagan with a personalized message: "Steve, thanks for all your continuing support. Ronald Reagan"

Yes, that's right—we had 200,000 signed photographs, with a handwritten note to each recipient. President Reagan was otherwise engaged, so the task fell to a group of women at the mail production company in Massachusetts, who earned extra money for the job. They were each given a sample of the president's handwriting to copy and executed a very credible facsimile.

What could be more exciting to the party faithful than to receive a personally signed photograph from the president? They loved the attention, and the response rate to this package was over 40 percent, as opposed to a typical response rate of 5 to 10 percent.

Don't Leave Home without It

Karl Malden served as the public face of American Express Travelers Cheques for 25 years—an amazing run for any spokesperson. His Travelers Cheques television ads were a perfect combination of excitement, news, and a compelling call to action. First you would see a thief stealing money from some poor, unsuspecting tourist's wallet or beach bag or hotel room. Then Karl would arrive on the scene looking like the cop he played in the famous television series *Streets of San Francisco*. He then looks you in the television eye and says, "This could happen to you!" And then the call to action: "Don't let a thief spoil your vacation. Get American Express Travelers Cheques." Little wonder American Express became the leader in this category, with 75 percent market share.

Mr. Whipple

Toilet paper is just not exciting. Yet Charmin managed to create a quirky character who was instantly memorable being eternally plagued by supermarket customers.

Pity poor Mr. Whipple, guardian of the Charmin display, who worked so hard to keep the product at its peak. Your attention was grabbed and you watched intently as Mr. Whipple caught the next culprit who squeezed the Charmin.

Mr. Whipple made Charmin seem so soft and enticingly squeezable, you felt as if you had to try some yourself—in the privacy of your own home, without being stalked by Mr. Whipple. Great call to action. A top-rate example of making one product stand out in its category.

Toppling the Category Leader with One Perfect Sentence

The ongoing fight for market share in the erectile dysfunction drug category is a great example of excitement, news, and a compelling call to action compressed into a few well-chosen words. As male Baby Boomers entered their 50s and 60s, they created a huge new market for a product designed to guarantee sexual performance. Pfizer was the first pharmaceutical company to capitalize on this need with the launch of Viagra, a purple miracle pill that would never let men down.

Viagra became an instant hit worldwide, quickly captured 75 percent of the market, and generated billions in annual sales. Products from rival companies soon appeared, but none were able to capture significant market share. Lilly Pharmaceuticals, the manufacturer of Cialis, was particularly vexed because they believed Cialis to be a superior picker-upper. They ran a continuous series of ads for months, with little impact on the market.

Then, much like this miracle product, a marketing phenomenon occurred. Embedded in the fine print required by the FDA for any and all erectile dysfunction drugs was this line: "If an erection lasts more than four hours, you must seek immediate medical attention." Eureka. With this discovery by a clever copywriter, Cialis changed its television and print advertising and made this line the hero. In print, it was the headline copy you couldn't miss, and on television, the voice-over ended each spot with the line as it simultaneously appeared on the screen.

Within three months, Cialis gained over 30 percent of the market and later climbed to parity in sales with Viagra. One sentence made the difference. Just one.

Eggs Overnight

Sometimes a simple visual (in this case, a logo) can create excitement and news on its own. Three years ago I was asked

by a venture capitalist friend if I could name and brand a new service he was backing—unique packaging that would prevent damage in shipment 100 percent of the time to prone-to-damage items. Many fragile items shipped by UPS and FedEx suffer quite high damage rates—from auto replacement windshields to light bulbs to satellite components. Billions of dollars are wasted, plus time for reshipment, along with major customer dissatisfaction.

The challenge was whether I could distill the issue and the solution into a company name and logo that would gain immediate understanding and recognition. I came up with the name and logo above—Eggs Overnight, with the accompanying tagline: "Not a yolk broken." Shippers of prone-to-damage items needed nothing further to understand that here, finally, was a solution that would save time and money and allow them to better digest their morning eggs and bacon!

Peter Lynch, Lily Tomlin, and Don Rickles

As an industry, financial services relies on the same old stereotypical images year after year in its advertising. We all want financial information and financial security for our families, but we are bored with the lame attempts to gain our attention.

Financial services also suffers from being a low-interest category. If you can't eat it, wear it, drive it, apply it, or play with it, it is of low interest. You never actually see or touch most forms of money, and that cash in your pocket really has no character or emotional bond.

If you want further proof of how tough it is to wow consumers with financial services advertising, consider that *no* financial services company has ever made it into the *Advertising Age* Top 50 Ad Campaigns of All Time list.

As Fidelity Investments head of retail marketing in the late 1990s, I was determined to walk away from the usual nondescript industry ad approach and inject large doses of personality into a campaign that would really shake up the business.

Anyone with a dime in the stock market knows who Peter Lynch is. And Peter has always been a major advocate of consumers understanding how to invest wisely. So, early in my days at Fidelity, I decided Peter would be the perfect spokesperson for a new campaign. He had never been in any form of advertising before. And Fidelity had never considered using a real person to promote their brand.

But I didn't want Peter to be just another talking head, although there are plenty of creative ways to make one person a powerful spokesperson. I decided to go into uncharted territory. Take a serious subject, money management, and create a campaign that would be as entertaining as it would be informative on issues like retirement, portfolio management, and the value of long-term investing.

Enter two terrific actors, both world-class entertainers, Lily Tomlin and Don Rickles, whom I paired one-on-one with Peter in a series of TV spots in 1998 and 1999.

The net effect was immediate. Employees loved this breakthrough approach. They were thrilled that Peter had "gone public" to represent the company and that he had two fascinating personalities to interact with. And customers and potential customers loved these ads as well. They were just so different. They were even fun to watch and listen to. People responded in huge numbers on the phone and online every time one of these ads ran.

Why Advertise?

Most folks believe that advertising dollars should be spent solely to launch a new product or service, build brand awareness, and generate leads. There is nothing wrong with these objectives, but by themselves they present an incomplete picture.

There are six essential reasons to advertise, some of which are not obvious.

1. *Motivate your "troops."* Advertising has enormous potential to excite employees and, if done well, will make them proud of the company and themselves. New ads should be previewed internally at various employee gatherings. This activity will create a buzz, and employees will then talk the campaign up with family and friends. Be sure to give each employee a schedule of what media the ads are appearing in, and when.

2. *Remind existing customers why they are customers.* Customers need to be reminded what a great company you are to do business with, an idea they would never come up with on their own. By creating awareness and jogging their memory, advertising encourages existing customers to take some action. Most "new" business as a result of general advertising will come from your existing customers.

3. *Generate new leads.* Everyone wants new customers, but prospects need information. Be sure to provide a web site or phone number that is very visible (most ads fail miserably at providing a clear call to action). Tell them exactly how and where to buy from you. A deadline always helps.

4. *Recruit great people from your competitors.* You can really tell that your advertising hit the mark when competitors' employees contact you about job opportunities and cite your advertising as the reason they did. Although they may not mention the ads, a spike in this kind of activity often can be traced to a successful ad campaign.

5. *Garner more positive publicity.* Industry reporters see your ads, too. Chances are you will be asked by many for an interview after the launch of a new campaign. Take advantage of their interest and go out of your way to be cooperative.

6. *Build the brand.* More awareness is always good. It is just that simple.

WHAT MAKES A BRAND SUCCESSFUL? HOW DO YOU MANAGE IT?

Branding has been around as long as humans have occupied the planet. From the day we are born, we continually compare ourselves to others until the day we die. Even after death, the beat goes on with tombstones and markers to eternally signify what our life represented versus the person buried in the next plot over.

Simply stated, a brand is a recognizable person, place, or thing. Our job as marketers is to create brands that are separate and distinct from similar products or services offered by competitors. It's all about differentiation.

The best definition of what a brand should do to be successful I attribute to fellow marketing book author, James Twitchell. In his superb book, *Branded Nation,* he states: "A brand is a promise that delivers an experience." I would add, "that delivers a unique and value-added experience."

Usually, a brand promise implies a guarantee of the product or service being provided. As I mention in Chapter 1, Roman marble merchants deserve credit for the first brand warranty guarantee. To advertise that marble was totally pure, they would tag marble slabs *sine cere,* which eventually became the word *sincerely* in English. In Roman times, it meant without wax—thus guaranteeing the marble you were purchasing was pure and free from cracks filled in with wax.

All successful, well-known brands are usually described in one or two words. They have achieved such a high level of awareness that you immediately identify what they stand for. A successful brand inspires you to love it, notice it, remember it forever, or even hate or fear it as in dictators and despots through the ages.

One of the most recognized and successful brands since the 18th century is the American flag. This icon can be summed up in one word: freedom. For the vast majority of liberty-loving people on the planet, it represents what humans live for: free will and a chance to pursue their dreams.

Truly great brands have four qualities in common. They are inspirational, indispensable, dependable, and unique. It is hard but not impossible for most marketers to deliver on the first two unless you market a country or a religion—though many caffeine-addicted friends of mine consider Starbucks indispensable! So striving to make your brand dependable and unique is the rallying cry we marketers should focus on every waking moment.

Brands evoke a wide range of reactions and come in varying forms. Some brands are "fuzzy" and mean different things to different people. Politicians are an excellent example of this ambiguity. To some, former president George W. Bush while in office was visionary, focused, principled, forthright, and a champion of freedom. To others, he was mindless, dangerous, arrogant, and a bully.

Frank Sinatra, who is hard to describe in a few words, is another example of a brand with complex and sometimes opposing traits. For many years outside his home in Palm Springs, California, there was a big sign that read, "Beware of Dog's Owner." Perhaps that said it all. Sinatra could be nasty, tough, unbending, and rigid. He could also be kind, loyal to a fault, and considerate. In all endeavors one could say he was passionate. Indisputably one of the best male vocalists of all time and a gifted actor as well. An enduring brand, but hard to pin down.

Generally, a brand can be described in just a few words:

Nike	Sports equipment
Coke	Cola
Marlboro	The cowboy/cigarettes
BMW	Cars with German engineering
GM	Federal bailout
FedEx	Overnight delivery
UPS	Package delivery
USPS	Snail mail
Obama	First black president
Apple	Innovative personal devices
IBM	Technology giant
Pillsbury	The Doughboy
Pentagon	Military headquarters
NBC	Network television
Mad Men	Hard-living ad guys
Paris Hilton	So yesterday
The Masters	Holy grail golf tournament
Four Seasons	Top-notch hotels
Denny's	"Grand slam" breakfast
Las Vegas	What happens there stays there
MIT	Techno haven for nerds
New York City	The Big Apple

How you differentiate your product or service from all your competitors is the whole focus of successful brand management. Fundamentally, brand building and management is all about the combination of these four marketing elements:

1. A compelling, unique selling proposition.
2. Strong visual brand imagery.
3. Innovative and reliable products.
4. Memorable and integrated advertising.

Additional information about elements 1, 2, and 4 can be found in later chapters.

Have a Unique Selling Proposition

You must be able to describe in a sentence or two what makes your business tick, what makes it unique, how your employees can fully understand what their best efforts produce and why, and what makes your company special.

A favorite example of a unique selling proposition comes from a dinner I attended several years ago. Seated next to the head of marketing for Harley Davidson Motorcycles, I asked the gentleman why Harley was the premium brand in the world of motorcycles, year after year. He responded:

> We allow overweight middle-aged white guys to dress up in leather on the weekends and ride a Harley through small towns and villages scaring the hell out of the locals.

That is about as succinct a description of a unique selling proposition as I have ever heard. Make sure you are able to communicate as well.

Insist on Strong Visual Imagery

Symbols or logos make brands last forever in our brains, a little like shorthand for the brand. At their best, they are overpowering and universal like the Nike swoosh, IBM for

International Business Machines, UPS for United Parcel Service, BMW for Bavarian Motor Works. My guess is that most car buyers today don't even think BMW stands for anything other than BMW. Combining their logo with a powerful, elegantly simple tag line, "the ultimate driving machine," BMW consistently comes out on top of the fiercely competitive luxury car segment.

You know you have arrived when your symbol is so strong that nothing else needs to be said. For many years, Shell Oil had the word *Shell* inside its yellow shell logo. The logo became so recognizable that eventually Shell dropped the word—it just wasn't necessary and in fact was redundant.

You Must Have Innovative and Reliable Products

Without an innovative and reliable product, all the best logo designs and unique selling propositions are for naught. A company must continue to innovate and not sacrifice reliability to stand out in the marketplace. That's why product development, as an initiative, is so vitally important and generally a key element of any marketing effort.

There are endless examples of product-driven companies. Certainly, the auto manufacturers come to mind as well as Apple Computer and the pharmaceutical industry. Innovation was clearly the case when the first airline shuttle service was started by Eastern Airlines—underlining reliability—something to this day only the shuttle services in the airline industry really deliver.

This is not a book about how to create products. It is about how to market them. But great marketing cannot overcome a ho-hum product. If you find yourself in a company with a mediocre product, get out before it fails.

Memorable and Integrated Advertising—Always

Most advertising on air or online is dull, and sometimes even stupid and insulting. Who can blame people if they are bored for skipping over commercials, changing radio stations, or leafing past ads in magazines. Your goal as champion of a brand is to get people's attention and deliver an unforgettable message through every appropriate media opportunity.

Simple as it sounds, the less people have to digest, the more likely it is they will remember what they have taken in. Combine brevity with a forceful message and you will have a memorable ad. The group running Lyndon Johnson's presidential campaign in 1964 understood this point when they commissioned ad agency Doyle Dane Bernback to show how foolhardy it would be to vote for his opponent Barry Goldwater, by creating the famous daisy ad. Considered the most effective political TV spot of all time, it opens with a cute little freckle-faced girl in a field of flowers, picking petals off a daisy and counting out loud and out of order: 1, 2, 5, 4, 7, 6. The camera closes in on her face, then her eye, which then fills the screen with black. A male voice immediately takes over with a mission control countdown: 10, 9, 8, 7, 6, 5, 4, 3, 2, 1, zero.

A loud boom is heard and a picture of a nuclear mushroom cloud explosion fills the screen. LBJ's voice comes on evoking W. H. Auden: "These are the stakes—to make a world in which all of God's children can live, or to go into the dark." The mushroom cloud turns into a firestorm and Johnson's voice continues, "We must either love each other or we must die." The screen goes black, and white lettering appears: Vote for President Johnson on November 3. A professional voice-over says, "Vote for Lyndon Johnson on November 3. The stakes are too high for you to stay home."

Needless to say, the Goldwater team was not at all pleased and succeeded in pulling the ad from the airwaves, which just generated more publicity for the ad.

A more contemporary example of memorable advertising was the long-running campaign in the Northeast for Champion Mortgage in the 1990s. Targeted at people who needed loans but had fair to poor credit ratings, Champion made their ads very straightforward, with a hard-hitting message that came right from the top. Their spokesperson, the company founder, ended every commercial with the promise, "When your bank says no, Champion says—YES!" That line and the 800 number were all you needed to know. And the line was everywhere, integrated into all television spots, print ads, brochures, pamphlets, loan statements, T-shirts—you name it.

Always a step ahead and often leaps ahead of their competition visually, Apple creates the most engaging advertising of the past 10 years in large part due to the Steve Jobs genius in making Apple a product-driven and marketing-driven company. This genius was evident when Apple introduced their iPod personal music device in 2001. They created a visually stunning campaign that utilized brilliant techno colors as backdrops to show the product in action on silhouettes of human figures in motion.

No matter who you were, what part of the planet you hailed from, whatever your age, you understood what the iPod was all about the instant you saw ads in print or on TV. They are so simple, so visually compelling, you had no

choice in the matter—your eye was immediately drawn in. To date, over 250 million iPods have been sold.

And who can forget the more recent "Mac versus PC," dork versus hip guy, simple yet riveting TV spots or the success of iPhone and iPad campaigns. Each is a prime example of the power of a minimal message, where visual images tell the product story a million times better than words.

As you can see, brand management need not be complicated or require you to read thick tomes with charts and graphs showing the life of a brand. Branding is not made up of scientific principles, like physics. Successful brand management comprises the four elements described earlier. If you stay focused on how to excel at each, you and your brand will stand to prosper. Marketing successfully is all about simple ideas brilliantly executed that reinforce your brand image.

CHAPTER 4

HOW TO CREATE A UNIQUE SELLING PROPOSITION

No matter what the marketing landscape looks like when you read this book—in 2011 or 3011—*every* company needs a clearly stated or visually obvious unique selling proposition (USP). It can take the form of a short mission statement or a tagline that resonates with employees and consumers. Sometimes it can even be just a visual representation of the product or service. A term most ad historians credit to legendary adman Rosser Reeves, a solid USP still remains the best way to differentiate your brand from the competition.

Federal Express is an example of a company so closely aligned with its USP that they really are one and the same. It all started with Fred Smith's brilliant concept, one that his business school professor said would never work. In the mid-1970s, Fred put together a business with a few leased Falcon jets and a great ad campaign created by Ally & Gargano: "When it absolutely, positively has to get there overnight." And thus, an enduring USP was born to live on as the Federal Express promise. A few years ago, Federal Express recognized the widespread usage of their shortened name, FedEx, as a verb to indicate overnight shipment of a package or document. The company smartly changed their official name to FedEx to trademark-protect this name.

It's hard to remember that through the 1950s and the 1960s the United States Postal Service dominated package delivery. What they completely lost sight of was that their USP of universal mail/package delivery was missing one critical element—guaranteed delivery on a certain date. Moreover, they lacked the vision back then and more recently of recognizing that no matter how much commerce is done via the Internet, packages still have to be delivered the "old-fashioned way"—by truck and plane. In fact, package delivery volume increases in correlation to the increase in online commerce.

So, it's not enough to have a unique selling proposition, you must have one that trumps the competition and prevents them from claiming a "higher spot on the marketing mountain."

Notice the 8-ounce glass Coke bottle. That unique shape over 120 years old is one of the most recognizable shapes on earth with or without the Coca-Cola lettering. Coke *owns* this shape. That's their USP. It conjures up the thought, "Only with Coke can you grab this bottle and quench your thirst. Recognizing the power of their singularly distinctive bottle design, Coke uses the glass bottle as the centerpiece of most of its advertising even though Coke in glass bottles is in limited supply in America and the rest of the world today. My guess is they will continue to use the glass bottle to appear distinctive in the soda world long after the bottle disappears completely from store shelves—a sad day for those of us who think the product looks better and tastes better in their glass bottle.

Probably the most powerful commercial USP of all time belongs to Marlboro, a brand that has maintained a worldwide market share close to 50 percent and has done so since the mid-1950s. The famous Marlboro cowboy represents positioning that spans more than half a century and evokes a sense of freedom to roam, to be myself, to do what I want when I want. He represents the mythology of the romance of the open range—the cowboy who looks the part and never waivers, generation after generation, that appeals to women as much as men, and works across all levels of race, income, and nationality.

Marlboro has created such a strong universal image that the cowboy sticks in the minds of consumers, even without ever appearing on a box of cigarettes or the carton they come in.

In fact, it was a very conscious decision to leave the cowboy off each box of cigarettes. Since the 1950s, when parent company Phillip Morris first launched Marlboro in the United States, the Leo Burnett agency has been promotional steward of the brand. The launch team, run by agency founder Leo Burnett, decided that it would not be right for smokers to actually crush the cowboy in their hands as they discarded each pack of cigarettes—in a sense crushing the legend and the dream of "free to do as I please" that the cowboy represents. Whether it was a stroke of brilliance or luck, it's hard to argue with the outcome.

For over 35 years BMW's USP is embedded whenever possible, as part of its logo—the ultimate driving machine. BMW is the only auto manufacturer that understands that a great brand promise should never be changed and should be integrated into every customer touch point. And they have been financially the most successful auto firm of all time. These two points go hand in hand. This USP is their reason for being, and the company strives to fulfill it in the design and engineering of their cars. There are probably no two companies more alike in their approach to consumers than BMW and Apple Computer. Like Apple, BMW charges a premium price and rarely discounts. They are very fussy about dealer service standards and close down dealers who do not meet them—unusual in the auto business. (Other auto companies close down dealers because of weak sales, not weak service). BMW gets away with saying that there is no better car on the road—BMW is the ultimate. Loyal customers seem to agree. Can you name another car tagline or promise off the top of your head? I can't either.

Three of My Favorite Unique Selling Propositions

These USP examples are personal favorites and represent a varied lot: a car dealer, medium-priced whiskey, and the Episcopal Church.

1. Car dealership sign in Boise, Idaho: "Fairly Reliable Bob's."

    Fairly Reliable Bob's is the largest car dealer in Idaho and, I am told, by far the most successful. I guess you could say: finally a car dealer tells it straight.

2. Canadian Club Whiskey. Canadian Club has made a big comeback from its former popularity in the 1950s and the 1960s partly as a result of the acclaimed TV series *Mad Men,* where it is prominently displayed and consumed all day and night by Don Drapper and his other Madison Avenue pals. *Mad Men,* which for the most part accurately depicts the ad business of that era, has also made the dress of those two decades filter back into mainstream acceptance. But unlike other products depicted, Canadian Club has

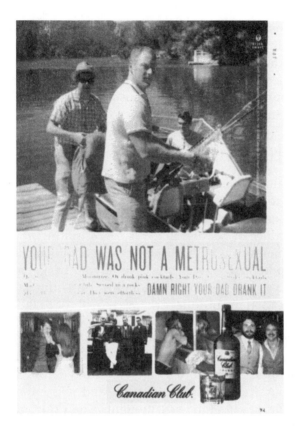

pounced upon its fabulous product placement by running a series of ads like the one shown here. The main message—"Damn right your dad drank whiskey cocktails"—reminds us that our dad's generation were manly men who drank potent whiskey based drinks and wouldn't be caught dead sipping a glass of white wine in their office or at the after-work bar or mistress's living room—perish the thought!

3. Ad headline for the Episcopal Church: "In the Church Started by a Man Who Had Six Wives, Forgiveness Goes Without Saying." This print ad ran about 15 years ago as one of a series that was created to turn

around rapidly falling church attendance. The campaign was very successful. It was also very controversial with the Church hierarchy and eventually was canceled for internal political reasons—just like what happens all too often in the business world, which is why so much advertising today is so bland and ineffective.

How to Create a USP

So how do you create a compelling USP? I promise, this effort is not even close to an exact science.

It often comes down to one overpowering idea about your product or service that sits there, staring you in the face. Sometimes it is so obvious that it is difficult to recognize its potential power. You have to step back, gain some perspective, and be honest enough to say—this fact, good or bad, is what my product or service really boils down to.

Sometimes a healthy dose of irony does the trick like the tagline created during the cold war for America's frontline nuclear missile and bomber arm—"Peace is our profession."

The best USPs often are discovered by accident. Epiphanies are not planned events, and it is important to capture those out-of-the-box thoughts when they occur. No one in the marketing business should be more than an arm's length from an "old-fashioned" pen and notepaper. I always carry these tools of the trade when jogging, going to a restaurant, a movie, a wedding, playing a round of golf, and so on. No matter where I am at bedtime, home or hotel, a pad and pen are handy. Sometimes the best ideas just come to you out of the blue.

Look at your competition and how they position themselves, and then work hard to find a completely different approach. If everyone else is selling cars, you sell service. If lite beer is touted as low-calorie, you sell great taste. If the competition says how cheap their product is, you might position yours as more expensive and worth every cent.

For a dentist friend (it is always good when your dentist is your friend), I came up with a tagline for his practice that is total fact, but something no other dentist ever thinks of: "You come first. Your teeth come second."

Another good example: The Chamber of Commerce of Summit, New Jersey, asked me a couple of years ago to come up with a tagline (USP) for the downtown shopping zone. My answer: "Summit. Everything else is downhill."

Bottom line: You need to zero in on a basic product fact and make it come alive as a compelling point of differentiation.

Key Features Only

So you have a great product or service to sell with many nifty features. Pick three of the most compelling and bring them front and center in all your promotional programs.

A long list of features only obfuscates the major reasons someone should buy your product. Long lists tune out the eye and the mind.

Own a car? How many features really mattered to you when you bought it? Probably price, the warranty, and handling.

With many durable products the major features should focus on ease of use, dependability, and convenience of service—will I get it quickly and at a fair price.

Whatever the product, three major feature highlights are sufficient to give the potential customer enough information to make a serious buy decision.

5

USING A SPOKESPERSON TO MAXIMUM EFFECT

Forget about Tiger Woods's well-publicized "Bimbo Eruptions," which cost him millions in endorsements and his marriage. The fact is that no sports star spokesperson is credible outside of the sports arena unless they focus on one and only one other nonsport product or service that they can genuinely embrace and endorse. A supporting fact— nine years prior to Tiger's mistress revelations he was hired as the spokesperson for Buick. And for the next eight years as Buick's pitch person their sales went down every single year. He wasn't even driving a Buick when he crashed his Cadillac in front of his Florida home trying to escape in the middle of the night. The point is that no one ever believed he would be behind the wheel of a Buick if he weren't being paid to do so. I will explain shortly how to pick the right spokesperson for your company and win consumer loyalty every time.

Most of the world's inhabitants look to a personality of some sort to explain their very existence—God, Jesus, Buddha, Mohamed, and all the other major religious figures revered over the centuries. So it should come as no surprise that a distinctive personality can make a significant impact in an advertising strategy.

The personalities featured in tremendously success-ful campaigns are legion. There are some who created or elevated an existing corporate personality: Colonel Sanders, Dave Thomas, Frank Purdue, Orville Redenbacher, Chuck Schwab, Peter Lynch. There are others who employed an already well-known face to distinct advantage: Karl Malden, Andy Griffith, James Earl Jones, John Houseman, James Garner, Dinah Shore, Jamie Lee Curtis, O. J. Simpson, and Candice Bergen.

Look at the world of financial services, a category in which all major players offer very similar products and ser-vices. A well-chosen spokesperson can make all the differ-ence. In the early 1980s, Smith Barney launched a campaign to build recognition of their brokerage business. They hired John Houseman, a well-known character actor, whose per-sonality exuded confidence and trust, a decision that was as memorable as the campaign they created. In each of the television ads, Mr. Houseman discussed a financial situa-tion that you, the viewer, should be aware of, and then com-mented on Smith Barney's expertise. He would always sign off with the line: "Smith Barney. They make money the old-fashioned way . . . they earn it."

This series of ads is one of the most successful cam-paigns of all time. People who were not even alive in the early 1980s insist they have seen these television spots and often can repeat the tagline even though it has been off the air almost 20 years.

The strength of personality is not to be underestimated.

Another example of personality defining a brand is American Express and their use of Karl Malden for 25 years as spokesperson for their Travelers Cheques division. This personality/product combination was so compelling that two things happened. First, during the initial years of the cam-paign, American Express built up and maintained a market share of 75 percent. Second, Karl Malden became known as the spokesperson for all of American Express. To the pub-lic he was American Express, even though he had no role in any other American Express advertising. Mr. Malden's persona extended throughout the entire brand by virtue of the power of his personality.

And you don't have to be a large company to make a large impact using a spokesperson. There are lots of success stories of regional companies building commanding market share with a highly visible and often highly entertaining pitch person. For a 20-year period Crazy Eddie's, selling all manner of hi-fi equipment, in the New York Tri-state area was ably represented by a paid personality named Crazy Eddie. More recently, Six Flags Amusement Parks uses a spokesperson who is a cross between Mr. Magoo and Crazy Eddie at half speed. The point is these two companies rose above the competition and got tremendous top-of-mind awareness on the strength of a character exhaling distinctive personality visually and vocally.

When asked about the use of a spokesperson, my answer is always yes. Why don't more companies do it? Some feel it will cost too much to pay the individual. Others don't like the idea of a personality selling the product versus the product selling itself. Unfortunately, most products are commodities and need some kind of booster rocket to get them into the consumers' orbit. Personalities can do that quicker, better, and more persistently than any other promotional device we have at our fingertips.

How to Choose the Right Personality

Choosing a spokesperson can be the single most important factor in a company's quest for better annual bottom-line performance. Whether you hire a celebrity or a company employee as your pitch person, you should insist on the following:

- *He genuinely likes and understands the product or service being promoted.* This point is *very* important. Real interest cannot be easily faked (Buick discovered that when trying to get Tiger to look comfortable in their cars). The best spokespeople are always comfortable with the product or service and show absolutely no hesitation to promote it. If there is a mere hint of "I don't care about this product" from a potential spokesperson, find another as that attitude will show through every time.

- *He is comfortable in social situations, and even enjoys press interviews and employee events.* If the person is awkward in group settings, does not care to meet employees on a regular basis, needs two bodyguards to take three steps in any direction, never wants to talk to the press—*forget* about using him. Also, don't expect most people and in particular actors to be good public speakers—they aren't. Ninety-eight percent of us, regardless of our occupation, dread public speaking, interviews, and talking off the cuff. Your potential spokesperson should be willing to get comfortable with the chore of public speaking. If she is not amenable to be coached in this area, drop her.

- *He is exclusive to your company—no other deals, period.* You do not need to hire this or that celebrity because four other companies did. You want someone unique to you—preferably someone who has never done commercial endorsements before and thus is not in any way overexposed.

- *He appeals equally to men and women from ages 8 to 80.* Sure, some products are just for women or just for men, but you never know when the other sex might influence a purchase. Kids influence parents, and even occasionally the other way around. Find someone who threatens no particular age group.

- *He must be agreeable to a fully integrated media role.* Some people want to do only television and not magazine advertising. Some do not want their images on your Internet site. Others refuse to record radio spots. Any of these "I won't dos" means this person is not for you. In the mid-1990s, when I ran marketing at Key Corp, a large financial services company, I hired Anthony Edwards of *ER* fame to be our spokesperson. He was a huge hit from day one. He fit all of the above criteria and was enthusiastic and cooperative about participating in all of our customer touch points. Here is the list of media applications that Anthony agreed to:

- Television, print, radio, various brochures and pamphlets.
- In-branch signage.
- Key Corp's Internet site.
- The voice of Key Corp's 800 number that customers called for all manner of questions, balance information, product queries, and so on.
- The cover of Key Corp's annual report, including a question-and-answer interview inside.
- Regular attendance at analyst meetings and employee-recognition events.
- Participation in several press conferences each year.

Anthony was a delight to work with and is a poster person for exactly the way these relationships should work.

The Remarkable Betty White

Fast-forward from the mid-1990s and Anthony Edwards to 2011 and the pleasure of working with Betty White, who turned 89 this year. I hired her to be the celebrity endorser for AARP, focused on exciting folks who have turned down AARP appeals for membership for years to reconsider.

Like Anthony in the 1990s, Ms White has broad appeal to all age groups and also ethnic categories. Simply put, she is universally loved and admired and has natural charm, poise, and a perpetual twinkle in her eye.

There is not a doubt in my mind that she will excite and delight millions of potential AARP members to follow her lead and sign up for membership as she admonishes them to "get over feeling old" and instead feel great about all AARP offers you to live your best life!

She will make this pitch on TV, radio, AARP's web site, in direct mail and e-mail as well as on the talk show circuit reminding audiences she is probably AARP's oldest and "best looking" member.

Nothing beats using the right personality at the height of her popularity when a perfect fit exists between her and the group she will speak for.

Going Hollywood

The very first step in finding a spokesperson other than a company employee is to seek the services of a top-notch commercial agent. Advertising agencies have access to the world of commercial agents and can generally guide you to someone you will be comfortable with. Begin by meeting face to face. Do not delegate this chore to your agency. *You* must establish an ongoing relationship with the commercial agent. Any agent worth a commission will want to get to know and be comfortable with you. There must be good personal chemistry, and all parties involved should share your commitment. Without it, the chances of success diminish greatly.

Once you tentatively decide on a personality, both of you should meet and discuss all aspects of the potential relationship. Again, do not discount personal chemistry. If this means you have to fly across the country and stay in Los Angeles for a day or two, make sure it happens. Use the criteria above and you have a real chance of major success for both sides.

A Word about Voice-overs

The craze today is to hire well-known personalities with pleasing or distinctive voices to narrate television commercials. This is not for the faint of heart. Annual fees range from

$50,000 to as high as $1 million. And although big bucks are put down on the table, most marketers do not get the most for their money, as they usually limit the voice-over to a single medium—television. The real payoff is a spokesperson who not only appears in your ads but also narrates off-camera. Use his voice on the radio and as your phone-service voice so that his participation in your campaign is truly integrated. Verizon for many years used James Earl Jones exactly this way.

Corporate Mascots

Corporate mascots are actors who portray made-up characters, created exclusively for your company. They are usually unknown to the public until they debut as your company spokesperson. Examples of famous corporate mascots are the Pepperidge Farm man, the Marlboro cowboy, the Maytag repairman, and Mr. Whipple. Properly positioned, these spokespeople engender interest, loyalty, and even affection.

Today, companies do not go this route as much as they did in years past. Instead, many just use models and unknown actors to pitch products without injecting any personality into the nameless spokesperson. They even forgo a polite introduction, such as "This is Anne Smith for Better Household Products." As you would expect, this nameless, flat approach is weak and not recommended.

Animated Characters

The advertising world's use of animated characters began in the early days of television with Speedy Alka-Seltzer, Mr. Clean, and Aunt Jemima, and expanded to characters like the Jolly Green Giant; Tony the Tiger; Snap, Crackle, and Pop; the Trix rabbit, and the Keebler elves. Other than Speedy, this lively group of characters is still in use today, over 50 years after they first arrived on the scene.

Probably the most famous and enduring of all animated characters is the Pillsbury Doughboy. He is worth untold billions in goodwill and embodies Pillsbury in the minds of consumers worldwide.

Animated characters are the easiest of all spokespeople. They are likeable, do not have attitude, usually avoid getting into personal trouble, and never turn off constituents with their political views. Plus, they don't need their own VIP trailers or dressing rooms, cappuccino breaks, or trips on the company jet. But, similar to their human counterparts, they do need contracts, they should be exclusive to a particular company or product, and they require the services of an excellent trademark specialist.

Companies with a serious message beyond biscuits and cereal can also benefit from the use of animation. Maybe because nobody likes to think about his own demise in an accident, or for any reason, insurance companies have invested a lot of their marketing efforts over the years centered on the exploits of animated spokescharacters. Everyone knows the gecko who uses wit and charm delivered on television with a vaguely British accent to convince you to call and see if 15 minutes really will save you 15 percent on your auto insurance. And Metropolitan Life delivers the point of the need for life insurance through Charlie Brown and his Peanuts gang. Met Life has used the Peanuts characters for 30 years and probably will for another 30. They are always tops in consumer recall, so why mess with the characters who made that happen.

Animals

Using animals has always been a popular way to get consumer attention and affection focused on a particular brand. It's no surprise to anyone that pet food companies use pets as their "spokespeople." Morris the Cat is among the better remembered. But the real question is: what brand was Morris representing? I can't remember. Therein lies the rub.

There is no question that cute puppies or cats or birds or horses that speak English get instant attention and often are remembered fondly for generations. A few years back in a Yahoo consumer poll of popular advertising icons in which 600,000 folks responded nationwide, the number two choice was the AFLAC duck.

Here are the top five most popular icons from that survey:

1. M&M characters.
2. AFLAC duck.
3. Mr. Peanut.
4. Pillsbury Doughboy.
5. Tony the Tiger.

It's interesting that all but the duck have peddled their respective products since the 1950s and are as popular today as they were 50 years ago, which underlines another reason why companies choose to use animated characters or animals—they never grow old and cranky. They never die. They live in a never-never land in our minds.

Back to the rub in the use of live animals like the AFLAC duck. People love the duck but don't know what AFLAC actually does. At this writing AFLAC is downplaying the duck in their advertising in an attempt to better explain the services they provide. So animals can be tricky. The more you can embed them into the actual product or service message, the more likely you can hit the correct balance between cute icon and what you actually do for consumers.

The Deceased

Deceased people work as spokespeople, too, but only if the fit is unique, realistic, and done in good taste. And long-gone dead people are way better than the recently departed—think George Washington, not George Plimpton. In general, though, this is a tricky category and 95 percent of the time not the right approach to take. That said, there have been a few campaigns over the past 30 years in which the use of the deceased has really made a big impact. The most effective was probably the long-running IBM campaign in the 1980s for its line of PCs with a Charlie Chaplin character as spokesperson. Chaplin played an everyman character in his silent films, the Little Tramp, and generated huge appeal as a simple person caught up in a complex world. Note: it's always easier to use a character one step removed from the personality himself, as in this case where the Little Tramp was the focus and not Charlie Chaplin as a person.

The Chaplin character was effective for IBM on several levels, principally because PCs were new to the market. First, it reinforced the notion that a PC was no big deal. You did not have to be a genius to figure it out; in fact, anyone could learn to use one. This was an important point to get across in the early days of PC availability. Consumers were wary and didn't want to be stuck with a newfangled machine that they wouldn't be able to operate. Second, the Chaplin character is viewed as simple and frugal, so despite the PC's cost the potential buyer could think, "Gee, I am not really being extravagant by purchasing one."

This campaign was truly brilliant and helped the entire PC category take off. It was a perfect fit between a long-dead movie star's character and modern technology.

What about Fred Astaire and Dirt Devil vacuum cleaners? These ads ran at holiday time for several years in the 1990s and then disappeared. They were cute and clever, but what really is the connection between being light on your feet and cleaning the floor? Well, none. Plus, the image of Astaire with a vacuum cleaner dance partner cheapened the memory of this great performer to millions of his fans. These ads did, however, get Dirt Devil noticed as a brand. Net net, this was not a bad launch strategy for a category with little general appeal.

A few years ago, Ford began a new campaign for its relaunch of the classic Mustang. Old film clips of Steve

McQueen were edited so he appears as a no-nonsense driver of this newly designed retro Mustang. Then, almost as abruptly as the ads appeared, they disappeared. My guess is that buyers for the Mustang skew quite young and none of this younger crowd have a clue who Steve McQueen was.

As I stated earlier, you must be careful with spokespeople who can no longer speak for themselves and have clearly never used the current-day version of the product or service. With the exception of the IBM effort, where a live person imitated Chaplin's character—thus two degrees of separation from the dead actor—showcasing the deceased amounts to shocking people into paying attention to your message. The shock part works, at least with those who remember or have read about the deceased character in question. What this shock leads to could be good, bad, or indifferent for your product. It's definitely risky business.

There is an agency in Los Angeles that specializes in representing famous deceased people through their heirs. This group, the Roger Richman Agency, is the right place to contact if you have any desire to pursue this approach.

But What if My Spokesperson Does Something Really Bad?

I mentioned O. J. Simpson and Tiger Woods earlier. The O. J. situation is more instructive since he was so closely identified with Hertz for so long. For many years he was a very strong and likeable personality as Hertz's worldwide spokesperson and did his part to help them remain number one in the car rental industry. Then the murders and the trial. What happened? Hertz acted swiftly and immediately canceled O. J. and all promotional traces of him. Guess what. No harm done at all, other than the loss of a sterling personality. So don't be afraid to use people just because there is a risk of their image becoming tarnished at some future date. If trouble happens, just move on. Consumers will, too.

CHAPTER 6

KILL ALL ART DIRECTORS (WELL, NOT LITERALLY)

It seems as if there has been a conspiracy among art directors ever since paper was invented to create ads that are impossible to read. First they pick the smallest, hardest-to-read type and then go one size smaller. If that doesn't make reading hard enough, they will throw in some white reverse type to seal the deal.

You might think of this problem as the "23/63 effect" in which scads of 23-year-old art directors create ads that they fail to remember must be read by scads of 63-year-olds.

Art directors are not evil people and, in fact, they would like their ads to be seen. *Seen* is the operative word here. Their primary focus is on how the ad looks, from a design standpoint. Its readability is not on the radar screen. Art directors waste billions of marketing dollars year after year on "eye tests" that don't work. Yes, billions.

Pick up any magazine and try to read the ads. The vast majority, say 90 percent, are in sans serif type (type without feet), with a typeface so small that your eye really cannot adjust. And, of course, you and I make a point to try to read the ads. Think about the average reader.

When a person picks up a promotional letter or brochure or skims over an ad in a magazine or newspaper, his eye moves at about 100 miles an hour. What is going to stop the eye dead in its tracks? Certainly, a clever headline that is easy to see will slow it down and may even stop it for a split second. In that second, the eye scans the rest of the ad and tries to focus on what to read next. If the rest of the ad is in mice type, the likely outcome will be to move on or, in the case of a direct-mail piece, toss it into the circular file.

The Web is hardly immune from the readability challenge cited above. Type tends to be crammed and body copy very small and, of course, sans serif type is used with abandon. After all, it's usually the same art director that works on Web ads as well.

Your job, dear reader, is to give your ads *every* chance of being read and acted on. Small type is the enemy. Sans serif type is the enemy. Reverse type is the enemy. And to not take control and insist on the art director's doing your bidding is a cardinal and unforgivable sin.

You don't have to take my word for it. Let's start with the fact that not a single English-language newspaper anywhere in the world uses sans serif type. They know better. And many studies have been done on type readability. One definitive volume on the topic is the 1995 book by Colin Wheildon, *Type and Layout: How Typography and Design Can Get Your Message Across—Or Get in the Way* (Strathmoor Press):

> Body type must be set in serif type if the designer intends it to be read and understood. More than five times as many readers are likely to show good comprehension when a serif body type is used instead of a sans serif body type.

Five Tips to Readability

1. *Always* insist on serif type for all your ads—just like every newspaper and mainline magazine on the

planet uses in their articles to help the eye connect to the words on the page. This book is printed in serif type. Almost all books are. Serif means that each letter is finished off with a little foot that helps the eye literally finish seeing the letter.

2. *If* you absolutely must use san serif type, apply it to bold headlines only.
3. *Always* refuse to use reverse type, which is simply impossible to read. Let your competitors use reverse type all they want. Let them waste their money on ads that have no readability.
4. *Always* think of your readers as 60 or older and focus on a type size that is kind to their eyes.
5. Whatever type size is first presented to you in an ad layout—insist on doubling or tripling the size.

The Great, the Good, the Bad, and the Ugly

I have randomly selected campaigns from newspapers and magazines during the fall of 2010 and spring of 2011, to demonstrate how difficult many of today's print ads are to read and comprehend.

Two Great Ads

In the earlier edition of this book I had no "great" category, but I am happy to report that despite very few print ads measuring up to a level of fantastic, I have found two that actually qualify.

Hyundai   Here's a company that thinks out of the box—a lot. Who would ever show a car ad today with no car? This is a terrific eye catcher to make the point you never have to worry about the reliability of Hyundai. Just keep flipping steaks in the backyard and relax. Another Hyundai ad is praised below.

Met Life Foundation Snoopy with no memory of life with his pals is simply touching and a powerful reminder of how devestating Alzheimer's is. This ad doesn't need a lot of words to make the point that we must find a cure. Beautifully done.

The Good

Harley Davidson   Harley is successful selling dangerous vehicles, aka motorcycles, to otherwise ordinary, risk-averse, aging Baby Boomers. The reason is that they position their product as "The Fountain of Youth" on two wheels. The headline of this ad is brilliant and right on the money, which makes Boomers who should know better part with their money. The one major flaw is the impossible-to-read body copy.

Jet Blue   This ad proves that words alone can create personality that positions a company in good stead with its audience. Remember during the financial meltdown in 2008 when the three auto CEOs each flew into Washington, D.C., separately on their respective company jets? The press had a field day, and so did Jet Blue, poking fun at the whole private jet privileged class. It made you want to book a flight with Jet Blue and give them a high five at the same time. So well done—even the white reverse type is at least large and basically readable.

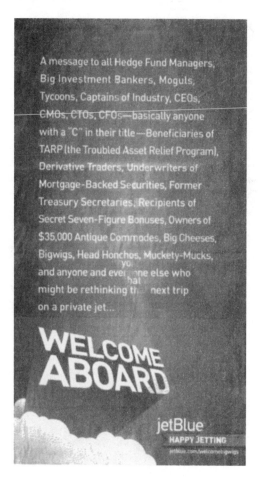

The Magazine Industry   With the tagline "The Power of Print," this ad to promote magazine reading largely succeeds in reminding us that we like turning pages and feeling paper whether we admit it or not. Plus, these folks get high marks for using serif type in black, not white reverse—thank the Lord and pass me the latest issue of *Vanity Fair.*

This is not the Internet.
Feel free to curl up and settle in.

Magazines don't blink on and off. They don't show video or deliver ads that pop up out of nowhere. You can't DVR magazines and you can't play games on them.

But you can take one to the beach, to bed or just about anywhere else and, chances are, it will engage, entertain and enlighten you in ways no other medium can.

Perhaps that explains why magazine readership has actually increased versus five years ago. The top 25 magazines continue to reach a wider audience than the top 25 prime-time TV shows. And despite the escalating war for consumers' eyeballs, readers spend an average of 43 minutes per issue.

What accounts for this ongoing attraction? Why do nine out of ten American adults choose to spend so much time with an unabashedly analog medium?

One enduring truth: people of every age love the experience of reading a magazine, even when the same content is available online. So curl up, get comfortable and enjoy the rest of this magazine.

The *Power* of *Print*°

Chase and Capital One Two banks that get it. That understand how to execute direct response print ads. Finally. Super large type. Clear benefit in the headline. Clear call to action, including the benefit of acting immediately. These ads are all the more impressive because most financial services ads are void of the very techniques both these firms use so well here.

Save
thousands on an
SBA Loan.
Then save
thousands
more.

UP TO $2,500 CHASE DISCOUNT + GOVERNMENT INCENTIVES COULD MEAN THOUSANDS MORE

CHASE IS AMERICA'S #1 SBA LENDER*

There's never been a better time to invest in your business with Chase. You could save thousands in SBA Loan costs from the government's Small Business Jobs Act, and you'll also get up to an additional $2,500 discount from Chase. When you factor in our lowest rates in years, it's no wonder more businesses get SBA Loans with Chase than any other bank. Act now. Offer ends December 31, 2010.

CHASE WHAT MATTERS
Speak with a Business Specialist at a Chase branch near you.

CHASE

Emblem Health   Emblem Health deserves praise for making its logo the hero in its first-ever brand campaign. A great technique seldom used. On top of that, the copy is generally readable and drives you to find out more—behold the call to action: "Find your plan at emblemhealth.com.

The plan that's designed
for your business.

To run a business, you need a blueprint for success. That's why EmblemHealth offers plans for small businesses, with premiums starting under $300 a month for individuals. Now that's a good layout.

EmblemHealth
The plan that works.

Coverage underwritten by Group Health Incorporated, Health Insurance Plan of Greater New York and HIP Insurance Company of New York. Refer to the policy for further details.

Find your plan at emblemhealth.com

Patron Tequila   A holiday ad with two simple words of headline that say all there is to say. And another cheer for complete readability with no white reverse type—hire this art
director for your business immediately.

Hyundai Hyundai is just smarter at promotion than any of its auto competitors. The luxury car segment doesn't need to advertise a long list of features—we expect the car to be fully loaded. What Hyundai does so well is offer luxury for less, and the headline says it all. And they actually invite you to visit their web site in the call to action. Few companies have the manners or knowledge to say "you will have a great experience if you come to our site."

Well done.

Metrokane (The Rabbit Corkscrew)   A fun positioning for a great product that makes popping corks a breeze. Cute phrasing of the call to action—"Where to go Rabbit Hunting." The only criticism is that the *huge* benefit is hidden in the body copy that should be highlighted for all to see—especially the majority of consumers who haven't bought a Rabbit yet. The benefit—opens bottles in three seconds!

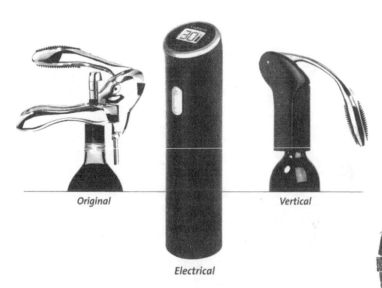

Original   Vertical

Electrical

Three ways to bring home a Rabbit®

The Original Rabbit® Corkscrew revolutionized the way we open our wine. It does the job in three seconds flat with little effort. The Vertical Rabbit "stands on its hind legs*" and also opens wine in three seconds with little effort. The new Electric Rabbit opens wine with no effort at all. And it has an LCD screen that shows you how many cork pulls are left in the charger.

So this year you have your choice of Rabbits. And they're all choice.

* "Now the Rabbit has been trained to stand on its hind legs..." *The Wine Spectator*

Where To Go Rabbit Hunting:
Macy's, Crate&Barrel, Sur La Table, Bed Bath & Beyond, Bon Ton,
Total Wine & More, Le Gourmet Chef, Kitchenkapers.com, Steinmart, BevMo!

metrokane.com

Bose   Bose made the first edition with a solid ad, and here they are again. Great play on words for their new exercise-friendly earphones. The white reverse body copy is actually fairly readable since they provide plenty of blank space between lines. If you insist on using sans serif white reverse type, this ad is best in class.

The Bad

Delta Delta wants us to believe that their new flat beds make sleeping a breeze. All long-haul frequent travelers know the beds are a joke no matter how flat because they are too narrow. Also, most folks fly coach, where no sleeping is possible unless you are good at cramped sleeping in a sitting position. Plus, the type, though not reverse white, is so small that reading the ad is clearly not a perk. Their new tagline is "Keep Climbing." How about leveling off and being truthful about the airline experience today?

Honda   Car ads come out in force at holiday time. Fine. So why make the pitch in mice type that no human eye can read without more effort than we will ever expend. The web site is called Shop Honda. I can't shop if I can't see it. The auto industry can ill afford to create eye-test advertising. Come on, guys.

Make the holidays even happier.

Xerox Xerox is a world-class company, so why is their advertising so amazingly poor and in this case utterly confusing. Is Mr. Clean their new icon? We have no idea what the heck is going on in this ad and aren't going to hang around to find out. And to make matters worse, Xerox's new tagline is so forgettable that I just hope they didn't pay too much for it: "Ready for Real Business." What the blazes is that supposed to mean? Is there unreal business out there in some satanic office park—perhaps in New Mexico where all the aliens from outer space hide? This tagline makes about as much sense. Hopeless.

Deutsche Bank   I am sad to report that apparently few folks in financial services advertising other than at Chase and Capital One read my first book—since most advertising in this category six years later is still lacking any reason for consumers to notice it at all. The brand promise here is absurd—Passion to Perform. That phrase would apply to, say, every company that exists. We all want to perform. And if they are so passionate, why not give me a number to call or a web site to go to? Instead, there is no call to action at all. Perhaps the Germans passion stops with a tagline.

UBS UBS is capable of decent print advertising when they have something specific to offer like a topical research report. This ad, however, with a reference to Thomas Edison and the light bulb, leaves us totally in the dark. Am I supposed to think UBS is baiting me to see them in a new way? I have no idea what they are trying to tell me. Their new tagline announces: "We will not rest." They should definitely not rest until they create ads that make sense.

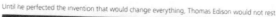

Until he perfected the invention that would change everything, Thomas Edison would not rest.

Until you see us in a different light.

We will not rest ✳ UBS

Pretty Dang Ugly

Bank of America   The background picture makes no sense unless you are a border guard in South Korea. The body copy, while readable, is as obtuse as the leadership in North Korea. Why compare this ad to North Korea? It's just as mindless. And, of course, there is no call to action. Perhaps a good thing, given that I have no idea what I am supposed to do after reading this ad.

We're more than your big deal banker.

We're also your every day banker.

From FX solutions in India,

to customized treasury services in Brazil.

Taking your opportunity further.

That's return on relationship.

Bank of America
Merrill Lynch

U.S. Trust Yet another financial services ad that meanders around and confuses any potential reader. The headline makes me scratch my head. The pictures are slapped together and create a big yawn. There may be something in the body copy worth reading, but no aging Baby Boomer with lots of money has powerful enough bifocals to even try. I didn't think it was possible to create a call to action in 4-point type. I was wrong.

WHAT IS

sharing lessons about wealth that you had to learn the hard way

WORTH?

As much as you want your wealth to help benefit future generations, you also want to know they'll be prepared to handle and manage it. For over 150 years, U.S. Trust has been helping clients pass down assets to their family members. And providing guidance through our Financial Empowerment Program to teach heirs about preserving and helping to grow those assets. It's another way we help you manage and transfer your wealth and worth. To see our rates, thinking on legacy and estate planning, read "Having the Talk" at ustrust.com/worth

1.800.U.S. TRUST ustrust.com/worth

U.S. TRUST
Bank of America Private Wealth Management

University of Michigan Health System   Who are these people
with their tongues out, and who cares? If you can read the
faint headline, it implies they are booing a football rival to
Michigan. But wait, the impossible-to-read white reverse
type says this is a cancer ad. Too bad no one will ever notice
the real purpose of this ad. Boo, Michigan Health System.

Expo Shanghai   Am I dreaming? Can an ad be this bad? If this is the best that China—the second coming of economic progress—can do, we are all very much in deep whale dung. Can't read the type. Don't understand who is doing what or what I am supposed to do. The worst ad since the Ming Dynasty. Period.

Colors

Red is the most powerful, action-oriented color, period. Think blood, think el toro. You want consumers to take action, right?

As a general rule, avoid using any colors in promotional materials that you see in most bathrooms: beige, light green, and blue.

It doesn't matter how rich or poor or educated or old your target customer is; everybody responds naturally to bright colors. That's the main reason the modern-day Santa Claus outfit was created by Coca-Cola in the 1920s to reinforce their corporate colors of red with white trim (a good trivia fact).

As for financial services, all the talk over the years about how green is a great color because it implies money and red is not because it implies "being in the red" is simply hogwash—whatever color that is.

The best contrast color combination for readability was discovered long ago by Western Union in the heyday of the telegraph and telegram—black letters on a yellow background.

If you never read the rest of this book, just tear out this chapter and tape it to your desk. Follow the advice in this chapter and you will dramatically increase the chances of your marketing materials actually getting red . . . er, read.

CHAPTER 7

LEARN FROM MAGAZINES WHILE THEY STILL EXIST...

There is a reason why *People* magazine is the most popular magazine of all time. Year after year, in good times and in bad, including the recent "Great Recession," *People* always maintains or grows in circulation. What's more, *People* generates the largest number of ad pages of any magazine in the world.

You can translate the success of *People* to your everyday marketing efforts, including brochures and other promotional materials, by utilizing the following four simple steps:

1. Use pictures of real people.
2. Use captions—*always*.
3. Write concisely; this is not a government report.
4. Leave plenty of white space on every page.

People magazine uses real people and so should you. For instance, showcase the actual people who run your company, manage the service, or who are customers who agree to be profiled. Avoid using paid models or stock photography of people no one knows.

People always want to know about people. That's why other successful magazines almost always show a person or

77

several people on their cover month after month, year after year. Women's fashion publications are one category that always highlights a female celebrity or model. Other notable magazines that tend to put intriguing personalities on their covers include *Vanity Fair, Rolling Stone,* and AARP. Their success begs the question: why don't marketing materials ever start with people on their front page? They should.

Billions of dollars a year are spent creating and printing brochures that get read by virtually no one. What a waste of time, money, and trees. You can dramatically increase readership by following the four points above and the following six tips below spelled out in a bit more detail.

1. *Put a picture of a person on the brochure cover along with what are called knockouts.* Knockouts are quick, one- or two-line highlights of the contents within. The person on your cover can be your spokesperson, your boss, a customer, or an expert in your company's field. Whomever you choose should be highlighted within the brochure as well, perhaps in an interview format.

2. *On the front inside cover, summarize the key takeaways of the brochure in bold and easy-to-read copy.* After all, why force the readers to go through the whole document to determine their interest? Give them the basic pitch right up front. This way, you stand a much better chance of their reading enough to make a decision, as opposed to putting the brochure aside "for when they have more time"—a time that often never happens.

3. *Tell the readers what you want them to do—on every page.* Call us at this toll-free number and/or visit us at the following web site. . . .

4. *Use a question-and-answer format within your brochure.* For two centuries psychologists have said that people see questions and subconsciously want to read the answers. Who are we to argue with the human psyche?

5. *Have a real contact name and return address prominently displayed.* Preferably, on the back cover.

6. *When potential readers grab your brochure, they will make split-second decisions about whether to read or toss it.* How do you stop them in their tracks and prevent that trash can hook shot? Always keep this thought at the top of your mind when designing a brochure. Think and act like you are the weekly layout editor of *People* magazine. And while you are at it, subscribe to *People* so that you get a weekly reminder of what "the folks out there" really like to read.

A word about photography and artwork: Most brochures contain abstract art or pictures of people, places, or things that have no bearing on the topic at hand. This stuff is often just filler that supposedly generates enough interest for the reader to thumb through the brochure to its conclusion. *Avoid* this approach. It has the opposite effect.

Do not fill your brochure with random artwork unless you are in the fine arts business. And make sure your photography focuses only on people or surroundings that are part of the story.

Consider a brochure as a short magazine, and do what great journalists and news photographers do. Copy these professionals faithfully in the creation and execution of your promotional materials. The pictures you use have to be an integral part of your story. Think what will make a potential reader pick it up with the same curiosity and anticipation that popular magazines generate with their fans.

Imagine Annual Reports that Get Read!

The same principles apply to annual reports. Thousands of annual reports are produced each year for companies and charities. Whether online or offline, most get little more than a glance on the 100 mph trip from the inbox to the file drawer or trash bin. There is simply no reason for this fate. Why not make your annual report interesting to see and read? Think: short magazine.

When I ran marketing at Key Corp, I put our spokesperson, Anthony Edwards of *ER* fame, on the cover of our annual report one year and Chuck Schwab the following year. In each case they were interviewed in a special section inside—Anthony on how he saw his role of spokesperson as helping families get a grip on their finances, and Chuck on the power of combining the resources of Schwab and Key Corp to provide terrific investment options for Key's customers around the nation.

Annual reports can even generate cash. At Citigroup I created a special shareholder promotional section from 2002 to 2005. Among other items, we sold over 10,000 red umbrellas each year that at the time represented the company's logo. These sales generated a small profit that more than covered the cost of the special section and generated goodwill among thousands of shareholders worldwide.

Who says annual reports must be boring beyond belief? A dull annual report telegraphs shareholders or supporters that you really don't care if they read it and consequently you really don't care about them. Let your competitors bore them to death. You can do better, much better.

CHAPTER 8

DO THE REVERSE OF WHATEVER GM DOES

This chapter should never have to be written. It's about a principle of marketing that is rarely employed yet absolutely critical to a successful outcome of any promotional campaign. Namely, offering the same product or service at the same time at all customer touch points. The two-word term is *integrated marketing*. No mystery here. Integration always generates better return on investment. Always. The only mystery is why most companies large and small have no clue.

I am picking on General Motors as an example of what absolutely not to do. At the writing of this book there is much backslapping among politicians and GM management over the successful recovery from near extinction brought on by the Great Recession of 2008–2009. And, yes, GM is in better shape financially due to a gradual recovery in worldwide auto sales and deserves credit for retooling and producing top-quality cars and trucks at very competitive prices.

The shame of it is that they could be so much more successful were it not for their lackluster marketing that wastes millions of dollars needlessly. Case in point was their Big Splash promotion in the early months of 2010. The then-chairman Ed Whiticare appeared in a hastily produced TV spot that ran constantly for six weeks and focused on him walking through a GM design studio. During his stroll he made two important points. First, if you bought any GM car or truck in 2010, you could return it up to 60 days after purchase with no reason given and get all your money back. Second, he ended the ad with a powerful brand promise reinforcing the 60-day offer: "May the best car win."

So what's a consumer to do? What I did was go to the GM web site to learn more. And what I learned was . . . nothing. The web site had no "may the best car win" theme or route to learn more or picture of the chairman as he appeared in the TV spots. No tie-in between offline and online. Nada. And what could have been a mega promotion wasn't.

It is incomprehensible that companies large and small still don't understand that whatever they are promoting at any given point in time has to appear in the same visual rendering at every customer and prospect touch point. In GM's case, they did a bunch of TV ads and nothing else—no web tie-in, no signage for their dealers across the country, and probably no brochures dedicated to the theme of the TV spot.

There is an important lesson here for marketers: all media must work together simultaneously in order to have a significant effect on the outcome of a campaign. It is way better to mount a two-month course of action that includes television, print, radio, outdoor, Web, and direct mail—all with a common call to action—than to commit to a year or any time period of just television spots.

An excellent case study is the MCI story—not the scandals that occurred after they became WorldCom, but rather the success of an incredible early growth strategy. A strategy that any company with a national footprint can benefit from, or if you have a regional presence only, where going from city to city might make more sense than employing one overall campaign.

Beginning in the early 1980s MCI transformed itself from a small, struggling, long distance alternative to Ma Bell to *the* other major player in the long distance market. Over a two-year period, they employed a blitzkrieg approach to marketing their residential and commercial services in a totally integrated fashion.

On a systematic basis, MCI went from major city market to major city market with an intense six-week multimedia blitz. This was marketing integration in a highly effective yet rarely done form, mainly because it takes so much coordination and preplanning. MCI also went back to each market for a "cleanup" campaign six months after the initial blitz.

The blitzkrieg war analogy is not accidental. MCI really thought of itself as waging war against AT&T. Put in a military context, they were a highly organized guerilla warfare unit at war with the army of occupation, AT&T.

Since they could not even remotely match AT&T's national ad budget, MCI basically fed off each market success, a strategy that allowed them to spend far less than AT&T. For a few million dollars in multimedia expenditures, MCI entered a market for six weeks, built up a customer base with new cash flow, and then leveraged the new liquidity to enter the next market.

Doing some simple math, if you spend $6 million in one market for six weeks, you have an impact of almost $52 million annualized. With this kind of penetration, consumers will remember ads for many months after they have run—especially if the creative and product offer are strong and memorable. In MCI's case their offer was simple and effective: for the same phone time, you will save a bundle using MCI versus AT&T.

MCI presented this comparison very effectively by showing two side-by-side gas pump meters, one labeled MCI and the other AT&T. The camera rolled with the two pumps "filling up phone time" for different length calls, graphically making the point that MCI could clearly save you from 20 to 60 percent based on the call length and route. This visual comparison was used in all forms of advertising, in all markets, to make the same simple point over and over again: "MCI saves you money on every call you make. Ma Bell is ripping you off. It's easy to switch. Be a smart consumer and show Ma Bell who's boss."

MCI also excelled at building and keeping a highly trained and motivated staff that AT&T couldn't match. MCI made all their employees at all levels true believers in their mission and their products. All employees used the service and saw the savings firsthand. All of them were given stock options and stock bonuses at a time when most companies just handed out stock to senior management. All employees could articulate their core mission—to replace Ma Bell—an out-of-touch behemoth that was ripping off the American family and attempting to prevent normal competition in the marketplace. (Students of American history should see parallels here with how a ragtag band of colonists beat the British Army and Navy against all reasonable odds.)

The MCI troops were a lean, mean, fighting-for-a-noble-cause machine. And they positively infected MCI's new customers with the same "we're in this together" mentality.

MCI's early years were integration in its purest and most powerful form. Their blitzkrieg strategy extended to nonstop attacks on Capitol Hill and the Federal Communications Commission, activities that generated constant publicity and raised awareness of the need for reform in the long distance phone market. MCI even moved its headquarters from Chicago to Washington, D.C., to be closer to the legislative action and to show their commitment to facing the enemy head-on. MCI encouraged their customers to join them in this fight and on their monthly bills brilliantly reminded them of their savings versus AT&T on each call.

I worked with the management of MCI in those incredible growth years and have never seen a more dedicated, coordinated, integrated marketing effort emanating from every single employee every day. Truly remarkable.

The "Electronic Church" and How It "Outmarketed" Mainstream Religion and What You Can Learn from It

During the same period that MCI was trouncing AT&T, an unlikely group gained fame and fortune with some of the best use of integrated marketing I have ever seen. In the 1980s the TV evangelists came into their own, harnessing the power of integrated marketing, and made a spectacular increase in the size of their ministries. My Epsilon colleagues and I worked firsthand with almost every major evangelist in the nation: Oral Roberts, Jerry Falwell, Rex Humbard, Jim Bakker, Pat Robertson, and others. It was amazing to see these men in action.

All of them were star performers who had been on the preaching circuit since an early age. Although I am not a big fan of zealots, religious or otherwise, working with these fellows and their staffs made me a believer in their genuine commitment to doing good deeds in the fields of health and education, and their devotion to the followers who provided the funds to make it all happen.

These preachers shared another very important trait: they totally understood integrated marketing inside and out. For starters, they knew how to make themselves compelling spokesmen. They also knew how to entertain their audiences and consistently focused on their unique selling proposition: "We are all children of God put on this earth as sinners and yet able to achieve eternal life if we ask His forgiveness and seek His blessings." Hard to argue with a USP that promises a pass into heaven for going along with the program!

Similar to the MCI situation, there was a large untapped audience in America looking for a good deal. In this case, the core audience was about 3 to 5 million 65-and-older women and men who could not or did not participate in their local church activities. For some, it was health problems that kept them housebound. For others, it was just too far to drive to the nearest fundamentalist church. Often, the local preachers were boring and uninspiring. Add to this core audience another 20 to 30 million born-again Christians, and therein lies a market waiting to be excited by a better offer, one far more compelling than traditional church "marketing."

Through the miracle of television, the top preachers were incredibly successful and collectively raised billions of dollars for their schools, hospitals, churches, overseas missions, and various pet projects. This accomplishment was based on two actions established churches could not perform:

1. They used the power of television to come directly into every home and provided real entertainment in the name of God—great singing, great acting, great fund-raising.
2. They stayed on message through a coordinated, round-the-clock media effort. Oral Roberts, for instance, had a twice-weekly television show, a daily radio show, frequent television specials, books, records, and weekly newsletters, all with the same message: "Tell me your troubles, your sins, your ailments, your concerns for you and your family and friends, and I will personally pray for you and them over and over again. And, of course, to keep my ministry going so I can keep praying for sinners and save souls, send me whatever you can spare as often as you can.

The Roberts Ministry spent millions to build, refine, and invent new and creative ways to harness the computer to maintain detailed records of the millions who responded to their on-air 800 numbers and direct mail. They hired the best database experts on the planet, my company at the time, to give them complete state-of-the-art computer letter capability. In a matter of days after a follower called or wrote in, a letter would be sent highlighting the details of their individual situation and offering what actually amounted to a one-on-one prayer session.

Even today, 30 years later, with the Internet and social networking creating vast and fast digital correspondence, few organizations, church or otherwise, respond to the consumer like Oral and other preachers were doing in the 1980s. And so-called organized religion never knew what hit it and still today is unable to marshal the resources to serve those who wish to call, write, or e-mail and receive rapid personal attention in return.

Clearly, for marketing to run on all cylinders and blow away the competition, all media have to work together, all the time. Be careful not to send confusing or contradictory messages. Colleges do this all the time. They mail glossy alumni bulletins showing the campus in all its brilliance and at the same time send fund-raising letters that stress their financial condition. What message are you supposed to believe?

Be sure ongoing public relations, internal employee communications, and customer communications are added to the mix. And remember, the media "song book" has to be the same for every point of contact with employees and customers to truly make an impact.

LESS IS MORE—NOW MORE THAN EVER

Americans for the most part are overcommunicated at every turn. Every company wants consumers to see their TV ads, spend time on their web site, and look at and open an endless stream of e-mails or mobile alerts. And fellow consumers are messaging and texting and on-the-go calling each other billions of times a day. *Information overload* used to be an academic term college professors used to describe the future. We are living in that future.

A long time ago in an ad agency that knew what it was doing, there was a resident genius who said every human who has lived cannot compute more than three features at one time. The agency was Ted Bates, and the "genius" was Rosser Reeves. Even perhaps God got it wrong when he delivered the Ten Commandments to Moses. We might remember the Commandments better if there were just three of them plus seven additional points for further consideration.

And two features are even better than three.

Not a single American male who drinks beer will ever forget "Tastes great, less filling" for Miller Lite beer. Or for that matter Cialis's just one "feature": "If an erection lasts more than four hours, seek immediate medical attention." All the other points about Cialis and Viagra are hard to remember. Does it last 24 hours? 36 hours? Does it always work? Does it affect high blood pressure? But, we all remember the four-hour warning.

It seems pretty obvious that for your product or service to stick in the consumer's mind you have to get to the point quickly with one major benefit and drill that point home at every customer touch point—and do so forever. "A diamond is forever," "the ultimate driving machine," "come to Marlboro country"—these three taglines have been in use 62 years, 41 years, and 45 years, respectively. And all three companies, De Beers, BMW, and Marlboro, are the leaders in their industries. Can you say the same about your singular brand promise? I doubt it. Today, companies throw taglines around like they are Jeopardy questions that appear for an instant and then are gone.

Too Many Choices Are Too Confusing

I said in my last book and earlier in this one: *never* change a great tagline. Never, never, never.

Back to Reeves's point—if you need more convincing there is plenty of scientific research that shows again and again that too many choices confronting consumers just serve to overwhelm them and they react by not responding at all. There is a famous study that Malcolm Gladwell lectures on regarding a supermarket that offered free samples of various jams during weekend shopping hours. Whenever the supermarket set up a sample table of 3 different jams, a steady stream of shoppers would stop at the display and sample the 3 jams. But when the store offered 10 different jams, just one or two shoppers stopped at the free sample table, and when 20 jams were on display, not a single person cared to stop and try any of the jams.

Many industries fall into the trap of generating long lists of features about their products that serve to confuse rather than focus potential customers on why they should make a purchase.

Automakers offer long lists of options and features. Credit card providers do the same. With cars, what potential buyers really want to know is: am I getting a great price, excellent financing terms, and a "cradle-to-grave" warranty. When people consider applying for a new credit card (assuming anyone on the planet needs another), the purchase decision boils down to: is there a fee and, if so, why; what is my credit limit; and what interest rate may I have to pay? Everything else such as travel offers, retail tie-ins, and even reward programs are basically background noise.

The folks who really understand the less-is-more approach to selling are the luxury goods merchants. For instance, if you are selling a pair of alligator shoes for $2,500, what can you say other than the price is outrageous and if taken care of they should last for a good while. Same with $10,000 watches. Most high-end clothing providers just show the garment and leave it at that.

Even the airline industry understands that, when all is said and done, the one item that sells seats is price. What type of plane they provide and the service or lack thereof is much less important.

Small businesses in particular often fall into the trap of thinking they must list every possible feature of their product or service in mind-numbing detail. Financial services companies also are guilty of endless copy describing their deposit or lending products or how their investment advisers will work on your behalf.

The worst offenders in the "let's kill the potential customer with knowledge" game are consulting companies, large and small, that offer employee training, or information technology (IT) support, or process improvement schemes of one sort or another. Their web sites and brochures go on and on and on in endless paragraphs that often fill entire pages and never get to the point. The point in this case is: what people expertise am I buying and what will it likely cost? These companies almost never show the real product—the consultants, along with their credentials, that are available for hire.

Particularly in a weak economy, consumers are not in the mood to spend a lot of time and energy trying to decode long lists of product or service benefits. They want to know the value proposition up front in large type and clear language. Even better if you can truthfully claim the lowest price and same or better quality than your competition.

Who does this approach well?

Geico does, as their TV and print ads show with a crystal *clear* message: "15 minutes could save you up to 15 percent on your car insurance."

Giant Walmart doesn't beat around the bush. It simply states, "Save money, live better."

Some companies choose to protect their premium price and positioning such as Stella Artois beer with their tagline: "Perfection has its price." Sure, they will always cost more than mass-produced beer, but beer is a basic pleasure and loyal followers will keep buying a better-tasting beer even in hard times.

It's as Easy as 1, 2, 3

A simple technique that really works to draw consumer attention to your primary product/service features is to number them—1, 2, 3. Numbers draw the eye's attention—especially if they are large and few in number. Most marketing practitioners completely ignore the psychological power of this technique in action. Use it every time you are promoting your business and you will achieve far greater readership than you have experienced before and most likely greater response as well.

And remember, an advertising headline can always be strengthened by injecting a numeric as in "six easy ways to lose 30 pounds quickly" or "four ways to save up to 20 percent every time you shop at _____."

The bottom line on getting consumers to pay attention to your promotion and not the other guy's boils down to human psychology and common sense. When we are infants, a fundamental form of learning is counting up to 10 with our two hands. We get this "training" over and over with parents and grandparents and babysitters repeating rhymes and counting on our fingers with theirs. This focus on 1–2–3, 4–5–6, never goes away. It is coded in our brains to stay. And as we enter school we get year after year of counting numbers as a core part of our education. Marketers just need to reinforce what we do naturally— counting off numbers, the fewer the better, while allowing the consumer to see the whole deal at a glance: "Why, it's as easy as 1, 2, 3."

It seems self-evident that numbering features and benefits organizes them for easy reading. This technique should be standard operating procedure on all Internet web site home pages. My rough guess is about one-tenth of 1 percent of home pages among the 40 million publicly accessible web sites use numbers to organize the home page information for easy-on-the-eye reading and thus retention. Crazy when you think of how far technology has taken us and yet how far we have strayed from organizing the digital world for clear and concise readability. There is still time—just take my advice in this chapter.

CHAPTER 10

THE THREE MOST IMPORTANT CUSTOMER LESSONS—ESPECIALLY FOR THE DIGITAL AGE

Lesson One: People Renew the Way They Are Acquired

This "law of marketing" happens about 98 percent of the time. So you do want to pay attention to this most human of human behaviors.

If you liked that first Big Mac, chances are you will have another and another, assuming they are consistent in look, taste, and, yes, even feel. The fast-food industry is a prime example of this customer axiom. Customers return because they have the same eating experience every single time.

However, the auto industry has not always paid attention to this rule. Practically every car manufacturer has had new car dreams dashed by altering the original design that brought the customer in the door in the first place. Some readers will remember the original Ford Thunderbird. It was a beautiful, new sexy addition to the Ford lineup and generated many new customers addicted to its sporty look. After almost 40 years of grim style changes and poor sales, Ford realized its design tinkering was a disaster and, too late, tried to go back to where it began. Chevy Corvette fared better right from the beginning by sticking close to the original Sting Ray design and keeping its high horsepower intact.

Chevy as a brand created a new ad campaign in 2010, with the theme: "Chevy runs deep." The gist of their message is that Chevy has been close to the pulse of America since the dawn of the automobile and still is today. Consumers should buy a Chevy because it is genuine to the values and aspirations of every generation of Americans. It is a solid campaign and wants us to "renew" our interest in a car line with history and heritage that will never alter from its roots.

It's worth noting that in early 2010, before the "Chevy runs deep" campaign launched, Chevy tried to convince us all that we should always say Chevrolet and not Chevy. It was smart that they dropped that request after noting the only folks who wanted the longer brand name to remain were the suits in Detroit.

Every product or service conforms to this customer renewal law. Clothing, drugs, dog food, toilet paper—nothing is immune to the law of customer renewal. There is even some evidence that many people who marry for a second or third time continue to marry people with the same characteristics as their previous partners. Italy has the lowest birth rate in the world and has for some time. Why? Italian men are so pampered by their mothers that they just settle into mom's home and care and literally never leave—talk about renewing the way you are acquired!

Bottom-line point: no matter what you sell, the successful renewal offer is one that is similar to, or better than, the offer the customer responded to originally. If your service has an annual fee, it is very hard to raise that fee without a lot of customer fallout.

Finally, media channels are not immune to how consumers like to respond. Many consumers, especially in America, like receiving mail and catalogs and responding to offers through the mail. And many millions prefer doing most everything they can online or with their mobile device. Put another way, it is very hard to get a hard-core online user to respond to "snail mail."

Lesson Two: The Most Critical Time in a New Customer's Relationship Is Right after Her Immediate Purchase

Psychologically, all new customers require some kind of reinforcement: they need to know they did the right thing by purchasing your product or service. It is your job to alleviate that postpurchase anxiety and make customers feel good about their transaction. Right away.

With e-business, it is very easy to send an e-mail thanking each customer for his purchase as soon as you receive a record of it. Think confirmation and thank you wrapped up in one e-mail response. Most companies doing e-commerce do just that. And in today's marketplace, every company, regardless of size, should be capturing every new customer's e-mail address every which way they can. It's a bit amazing that, with the advent of a new decade in 2011, the average capture rate of customer e-mail addresses is still hovering around only 17 to 20 percent.

Therein lies a challenge that marketers have done little to overcome. What will set you apart from your competition is to reinforce to a brand new customer, with as much humor and candor as you can, that you can serve them better and environmentally greener if they visit your web site and take a few minutes to fill out an online preference survey. By doing so you will know when to contact them and about what, and not flood their digital inbox with too much "unwanted" e-mail traffic. Most consumers will appreciate your desire to serve them and not send endless amounts of e-mail because it is easy to do.

By all means, give the customer the option of indicating when they wanted to be alerted by you about a specific product or service or price or special sale and so on.

Remember, Time Is Your Enemy

What about a real letter or postcard thank you in the digital age? Doing so is customary if the purchase includes a tax deduction unless the customer has specifically indicated they don't want a paper confirmation. Beyond a tax require-ment, a paper thank you is necessary only if you can't send a digital one. Just remember, a letter or postcard works only when you send it immediately after the transaction. If it takes weeks for the customer to receive your communica-tion, it can look like you have some huge impersonal system that runs on its own time, not the customer's. Better to send nothing than to thank someone for their first purchase far out in time from the purchase date.

There are occasions where a letter delivered by mail and not e-mail is the most appropriate course of action even when you have the customer's e-mail address. Specifically, this action is called for when you need to apologize for a service lapse. And if you do, the letter needs to get to the customer within a few days or perhaps even be sent for over-night delivery.

My favorite story of what not to do with an apology let-ter happened way back in the 1980s to my former wife, Faye, who worked on the Dell Computer account for Chiat/Day, an advertising agency in New York City. Dell is head-quartered in Austin, Texas, which necessitated her flying between there and New York on a regular basis. American was the only major airline that made the trip, with a stop on the way in Dallas. Most of her flights went smoothly, but on one occasion, the first leg from New York to Dallas was severely delayed because of fog in Dallas. The plane circled and circled and finally landed in Dallas two hours behind schedule and too late for Faye to make the connection to Austin in time for her meeting. She had to turn around and come back to New York. Well, these things happen; bad weather disrupts air schedules.

About five weeks later, Faye received a personalized letter from American Airlines. The letter began with an apology for the delay of her flight five weeks previous. It went on to say that despite this weather-caused delay, American strived to get trav-elers to their destinations on time. As a token of appreciation for her frequent flyer status, they automatically credited her frequent flyer account with 2,500 additional miles.

Faye showed me the letter and I was impressed. American had all the data right. They took the time to apologize and provide some solace with extra miles that Faye never expected. It appeared to be a real class act. I said to Faye, "Gee, these guys have really done a good job to make amends for that nightmare flight you had last month." She didn't agree. "They are four weeks too late," she said. And she was right.

When to Ask for the Next Purchase

This section is mostly about responding quickly to thank a brand new customer. Ironically, the best time to ask customers, new or otherwise, for additional business is right after they buy something from you or pay off a long-standing obligation. I saw this approach work wonders at several banks I worked for. We set up a system so that several weeks before a car loan was to be paid off, we sent the customer a letter thanking them for their stellar payment record and offering to give them another loan for a new car with very little paperwork or effort on their part. New loans grew noticeably from this easy-to-do technique. Part of the impact was and is that virtually no financial instituion ever thanks a customer for paying off a loan. The customer is shocked and delighted! If you are in the loan business, you should definitely consider this approach.

A smartly run mail-order food company, Omaha Steaks, was the first company I know of to take a slight twist to delighting customers. When you call or go online, you are likely to see that because you are an existing customer, every item is cheaper than list price. They also offer daily specials that really are good for only a single 24-hour day—another simple and powerful technique that few companies ever get around to doing. If you can, you should.

Lesson Three: Forget Complicated Clusters and Demographics

There are endless books and studies and doctoral disserta-
tions on long-winded matrix descriptions of customer groups.
Most of it is so complicated that you will never be able to create a marketing program to fit the endless customer clusters,
as some experts call them, or even to identify these clusters
within your customer universe in the first place.

So let's get down to basics. Every company, no matter what, has five customer groups. Some might call these
the loyalty ladder or customer pyramid. Fine and dandy. In
any event, these groupings are easy to understand and have
behavior patterns that will respond to a well-designed marketing strategy.

1. *The Evangelists: they love you, period.* They are usually just
   5 to 10 percent of your customer base. And they cannot
   say enough good things about your company or product. And if you keep asking for the order, they will keep
   buying. Devotees that they are, they deserve all kinds of
   positive reinforcement, from exclusive "insider" communications to an onslaught of special offers. Special
   does not necessarily mean cheaper pricing, by the way;
   special means . . . well, special. Something your other
   customers do not have access to. After all, this group
   usually represents 90 percent of your profit.
2. *On the Fence: they buy occasionally.* They represent the
   majority of your base and are apt to be somewhat
   price sensitive or feel that you do not always have the
   best product for their needs. They require compelling
   reasons to increase their business with you—an exciting offer, a special customer service, a positive comparison of your product to the competition, or just
   something altogether new and different. The punch
   line for you here is: out of this group come the
   Evangelists of tomorrow. If you manage to do a good

job with only these first two customer groupings, your business will likely thrive and grow year after year.

3. *The Price Is Right: they probably bought from you once, responding to a solid price offer.* Most of these customers will never change and will only shop price. If you have the lowest price point on the planet, by all means tell them like Walmart does so very well. When marketing to this group, remember that price motivates them and probably nothing else ever will.

4. *Negative: they had a bad experience in the purchasing cycle, perhaps a frustrating customer service interaction.* A telltale sign of this customer group is they bought once and that was that. So just forget about them, right? Well, not necessarily. I know several organizations that are quite successful in converting some of these customers to On the Fence and even to Evangelists. Their technique is to send a very lengthy apology letter that addresses the customer's bad experience head-on and admits that the company is not always perfect: "Yes, we fail sometimes. We hate it when we do, but it happens. We are human, after all. Please let us make amends and be given a second chance." As noted before: If you receive a complaint letter, phone call, or e-mail, it is very important that your apology letter go out immediately after the complaint is received, preferably the same day.

5. *No Clue.* Yes, there are these folks on every customer list. They often do not even know they are customers. Perhaps they bought once by mistake or were given your product as a gift. Just make sure that you treat them like any other prospect. They are not really customers.

A Common Mistake You Should *Never* Make

Now that you understand who your customers are, it is time to focus on how to treat them. When someone identifies himself as a very good customer, the natural reaction of most companies, large and small, is to stop communicating with him. They erroneously believe they run the risk of irritating a great customer by sending him too many letters or e-mails with more offers. Of course, when you cease communication or reduce it from previous levels, your message being received by the customer is, "You aren't important to us anymore."

Do not fall into this trap. Remember, your competitors are still trying to get the attention of your best customers any chance they can. Most well-run not-for-profit organizations understand the importance of continual but appropriate communication with their best contributors. Their organization's health and well-being is based on constantly presenting their case directly to the people who can really make a difference financially.

It's a marketing given that most businesses exhibit the 20/80 rule: 80 percent of revenue comes from 20 percent of the customers. Fair enough. But not-for-profits go one step further and have determined that 50 percent of their revenue comes from just 1 percent of their contributors.

If companies do the research and really pick apart the 20 percent representing their best customers, they will generally find a 10/90 rule, which says a mere 10 percent of customers generate 90 percent of the revenue. That 10 percent is a group that most definitely needs special care, attention, and an ongoing dialogue. It is manageable enough in size for a team of your best marketing people to focus on.

Sometimes this dialogue takes the form of special service that companies like Fidelity, Schwab, American Express, Hertz, and retailers like Saks and Tiffany provide for their very best customers. For example, it can be a constant reinforcement at the point of sale. Barnes & Noble has a frequent buyers club with automatic discounts at checkout on every book or item purchased in one of their stores or online. They even charge an annual $25 fee and customers gladly pay it.

Or it can be a special add-on to your service, such as the way car dealers reward their best customers with hassle-free use of a courtesy car when their car is in for service. It can even take the form of communications like Fidelity and Schwab send their top customers: a special quarterly magazine with content targeted for their affluent lifestyle.

The more activity a customer has with your business, the more she should be recognized through communication, service, and/or price. Whatever the interaction, it should be relevant, newsworthy, and frequent.

Hey, But I Sell to Businesses and Not Directly to Consumers

I have news for you, then: business buyers are still consumers. They fall into the same customer categories and exhibit the same human behavior. The only real difference is that they do more transparent comparison shopping by often sending requests for proposals to a gaggle of possible providers. But how they reach a final purchase decision is not unlike their behavior with their consumer hat on looking for a new car to buy, or lawn mower, or laptop computer, and so on.

The Guthrie Lesson

In the early 1980s, the highly acclaimed Guthrie Theater in Minneapolis found itself in difficult financial straits. They signed on as an Epsilon client and wanted us to create their first-ever direct-mail fund-raising campaign to loyal season ticket holders.

As might be expected, Guthrie's management was nervous about the solicitation and just about came unhinged a week before the scheduled drop date. They called daily with a constant battery of questions: "What if some people complain?" "What if they write nasty letters back?" "What if we get subscription cancellations?" What if, what if. . . .

My response was a simple one, based on years of hard-won experience. Yes, I told them, you will get all of the above.

I can guarantee it. You are mailing to 50,000 people. You will raise a lot of much-needed money. And, yes, you will also get "hate mail." In fact, the more powerful the letter, the greater the number of disgruntled responses that will land in your mailbox.

"Is there a way to prevent this hate mail?" they asked. "Yes," I said, "the solution is to cancel the mailing and raise no money."

They went ahead with the mailing and continue their annual appeal to this day.

Lesson: Whenever you communicate with large numbers of people, you will hear unwanted comments from a very small percentage of the group. That's just the way it goes. Don't ever let a few complainers dictate how you conduct your overall communications program.

CHAPTER 11

LOYALTY REIMAGINED

Loyalty programs really got their "wings" beginning in the late 1970s when American Airlines rolled out the very first frequent flyer program followed by all manner of businesses launching customer loyalty programs ever since.

A lot has changed since then, especially with all customer touch points today able to track customer behavior at point of sale, at call centers, or online.

But one thing hasn't changed and it's an important constant to remember.

Customers Rarely Are Loyal

What I mean is they rarely think of your company, your product, or your service. They have a million other things on their minds from dawn to dusk 24/7. Most companies fall into the trap of thinking customers are constantly aware of their offerings and service. Just not true. What is true is that consumers think about a particular brand in short bursts that often last just a few seconds—every once in awhile. Like, when they have a specific need; for example, I have a headache—where is the Advil?

Except for a few complusive shoppers, nobody likes to buy anything unless they have to—they would rather hold on to their money and spend less time worrying about possibly outliving it.

Enter loyalty programs. Their purpose is to remind consumers that when they need to make a purchase, it will be more rewarding if the consumer always buys the same product from the same company and not its competitors.

And to stand above all your competitors, you need to have a unique feature or two to really drive home the point that *you* are worthy of all repeat business—not the other guy.

Example: In Chapter 2, where the elements that make up a winning campaign are defined, I describe the success of WorldPass, Pan Am's frequent flyer program. Although they were the last major airline to launch such a program, Pan Am garnered tremendous loyalty and increased business because they totally outshined their competitors' programs. The awards were better and easier to earn. The communications were compelling. The whole look and feel of the program was very upscale. And Pan Am customers felt appreciated and special.

While every other airline paid out as little as possible to mail announcement letters and monthly statements, Pan Am spent whatever it took to look like a "million bucks" in the mail. In the initial package, a complementary round-trip coach ticket was included, good on any domestic U.S. route for six months—with no blackout dates or restrictions of any kind. No other frequent flyer program had ever offered such a rich enrollment offer.

There was only one requirement. You had to fill out a reply form with your travel patterns and preferences, and pay the $25 annual program fee.

Yep, Pan Am was the first and only airline to charge frequent flyers an annual fee to enroll in its program. This action was unheard of at the time. Crazy, many pundits thought. They were dead wrong. The program flourished. Cabins filled to their highest levels in years. Participants gladly paid the fee.

Pan Am's experience illustrates the number one fundamental of a successful customer loyalty program:

The Program's Perceived Value Must Exceed the Perceived Cost

Over the years I have seen a lot of mushy loyalty programs where the value/cost proposition isn't clear. If customers can't figure out what the deal is, chances are they won't actively participate.

A prime example of positive perceived value centers around what American Express has accomplished with its card business. Back in 1984, they launched the Platinum Card, a quantum leap in charging for a piece of plastic. The annual fee was $300, and if the cardholder wanted a companion card, that was another $300. At the time, no other competitors charged more than $50 for the privilege of carrying their cards.

The Platinum Card was a winner from day one. It was elitist and available only by invitation. Very smart. It also promised way more service and card benefits, and it delivered. American Express pointed out very clearly that the card wasn't for you unless you traveled and/or dined out extensively.

Almost 15 years later, American Express came out with a Black Card. It has the same basic positioning as the Platinum Card, but with dramatically enhanced benefits for the frequent traveler and a service level unequaled by anyone in the credit/charge card business. The original annual fee was $1,000. Again, invitation only. Two years after its introduction, American Express raised the Black Card (they call it Centurion) annual fee to $2,500, but grandfathered all cardholders who were originally invited to receive the card at the initial $1,000 fee. As with the Platinum Card, demand for the Black Card has far exceeded supply.

Can you charge more for better service? A lot more? And build customer loyalty at the same time? Clearly, the answer is a big yes, *if* the value is seen to outdistance the cost. The perceived value of the American Express brand adds to the proposition and enables them to create these elite cards. With high charge volume and high renewal rates, the Black and Platinum Cards are financial winners for American Express and "must-haves" for every affluent world traveler.

With these two premium cards, American Express engenders very strong customer loyalty—so much so, they are the envy of the credit card industry.

Most Loyalty Programs Create the Opposite Effect

Yep. They either have very little effect or they prompt consumers to look for a better deal somewhere else. The fundamental flaws come in two basic forms:

1. It takes forever to build up enough points or credits to get a reward.
2. It's a 12-month program, and every December 31 the customer has to start all over again.

Probably the world's leading loyalty program expert, Hal Brierley, who has been a colleague and a friend for 40 years, makes a good case that loyalty programs that set a high bar for entry are really missing the boat. Speaking of which, he cites cruise loyalty programs as major offenders. Example: You and your spouse finally take your first cruise. You discover in literature and on board that you can get great cabin upgrades and dinner with the captain and so on, all beginning with your tenth cruise. In the meantime, just keep coming and spending and spending, and eventually something good will happen. Many folks just say the heck with it and don't even bother to sign up.

Even Starbucks, supposedly customer driven beyond belief, doesn't really incent its customers to become super-loyal over time. They offer the same old tired approach used by so many companies—in Starbucks' case, buy endless cups of coffee and get one free every now and then. A major snore that all the caffeine in the world won't cure.

What they should do is take a look at what Barnes & Noble does, which ironically has mini-Starbucks sites in many of its stores. Barnes & Noble employs a basic instant-gratification approach to their loyalty program. Consumers pay an annual $25 fee that entitles them to a 10 percent discount off everything they buy online or in the store. And that's 10 percent off any item on sale as well. Members are issued a plastic card with a member number. Forget your card? Your telephone number allows the salesclerk to verify your membership and issue the discount.

My only suggestion is they should tier the discount and at a certain level of cumulative purchasing, offer an even deeper discount.

The other issue with loyalty programs as cited earlier is: if they are annual, what's the point? Actually, there are ways to make annual programs sexy enough to hold consumers' interest. Two retailers that do that well are Barneys and Neiman Marcus.

Barneys offers annual payback in hard cash that can be spent only at Barneys. Their program has a great name: FREE STUFF. The one requirement is that customers must use the Barneys charge card to get purchase credit. It amounts to a 10 percent payback in cash for use the following calendar year for all charges made in the preceding year.

As in the Barnes & Noble program, all charges count from full-price merchandise to items on sale. Barneys smartly provides a simple chart that shows how many "free" dollars you will get on your FREE STUFF card based on how much you spend. When you receive your FREE STUFF card at the beginning of the next year, you have a year to use it.

Additionally, Barneys' monthly charge statement shows you how many FREE STUFF dollars have been accumulated to date. This is a very easy to understand and powerful customer loyalty program with a single primary benefit.

What about Neiman Marcus? They offer point redemption for merchandise at predetermined levels. Launched in 1984, Neiman's InCircle Rewards was the first heavily promoted frequent shopper program to reach out to customers and build shopper loyalty.

InCircle members receive points for every dollar spent on their charge cards: one dollar equals one point. Once shoppers reach the 5,000-point level in any given year, they can redeem their points for merchandise—a fairly low threshold, which is key to maintaining customer interest. Like the Barneys program, the meter goes back to zero every December 31 at midnight: there is no carryover in points from one year to another.

However, Neiman spices up their program by regularly announcing double-points days when every dollar you spend equals two points. They also provide special benefits and rewards for the wealthy loyalist who spends $100,000 per year, and for the ultra-wealthy individual who finds a way to buy $1.5 million dollars worth of what Neiman Marcus has to offer.

Is There Any New Thinking in the Loyalty Space?

There is, and it comes from my previously mentioned friend, Hal Brierley.

Eleven years ago he came up with the novel concept that consumers should be rewarded for their time. Not for purchasing but strictly for the time they spend doing something of value for a company—like participating in a product research panel. Thus, Research Now was born, allowing millions of people worldwide to participate in online research polls and get paid in cash or merchandise for the time they spend, which is entirely up to them. Research Now is a huge present-day success and handles more than 30,000 surveys annually.

A few years back, Hal also started a service called e-Miles. E-Miles is the same basic concept as Research Now, but it's not research. Rather, frequent travelers are asked to sign up and earn miles simply for looking at advertising online and answering a few questions about what they like or don't regarding the ad and the offer. The e-Miles member also can choose to buy the product or service offered or sign up for more information. It's a great way to earn travel points just for spending a few minutes a week looking at advertising.

An important element about e-Miles is that when a person agrees to enroll, he fills out a lengthy online survey about his interests, hobbies, family, hopes for the future, and all manner of product and service preferences. The new enrollee is told that he will have his own portal populated with offers targeted to him based on his survey information, and that he should check the portal regularly to see new offers that have arrived. Again, for each promotion he looks at, he gets paid in miles—just for looking at the ad and answering a few questions. Paying consumers for their time is a novel concept and long overdue. More companies should be doing exactly the same thing.

It's About Time

With all the technology distractions of life today, time for most folks is indeed a scare resource. And companies that recognize this fact and make it a mainstay of their strategy are more likely to prosper than those that do not. The whole reason for the amazing success of Google is that you can get information on any topic at any time in seconds. This is a transformational change that rarely happens in history. Google is the 21st-century equivalent of the invention of the electric light. It changes forever how we live and how we consume.

In many ways, customer loyalty today and tomorrow has morphed into wanting the right offer at the right time online or at least all the information needed to then go and make a purchase online or at a physical location.

I will use the U.S. Postal Service as an example of an entity mired in the last century and unable to grasp how to make time their friend instead of their enemy. Compared to Google, mail is a slow boat to China times 100. What the Postal Service has never come to grips with is that the digital age requires digital delivery solutions. Yes, there is some physical delivery that is very important. But that is not mail. It is package delivery, which, unfortunately, the Post Office has ceded mostly to UPS and FedEx and thus cannot count on that business to bail them out of a long, painful decline in mail volume with no end in sight.

What our postal pals should have done was create a digital online mailbox for every American with a Social Security number, and then offer to create a personal portal, just like e-Miles has done, so that millions of Americans can receive digital mail based on their specific lifestyle and interests. The postal folks could charge companies handily for this service, which is void of 99 percent of the labor and transportation costs that plague the mail delivery business. Everybody wins in this scenario. It is a shame they can't get their act together and ensure a bright future versus a bleak one.

What Customers Really Love Is Real-Time Personalized Service at Every Point of Sale

The simple fact is that you can generate amazing customer loyalty by highly encouraging customers and prospects to fill out an online preference survey about how they want to be serviced by your firm. You then use that information to manage all aspects of your interaction with the customer in every channel they happen to come to—physical store or location, call center, your web site, by e-mail, and increasingly by mobile phone. Two companies that excel at this approach are Sears and Hilton Hotels. In both cases, when a customer makes contact through any channel, the customer is greeted with an offer or service-level recognition based on their profile that is kept current in real time worldwide. If they take advantage of a particular offer, seconds later another offer that fits their profile will be available on every channel they might happen to utilize. It doesn't get better than this from a service perspective.

Loyalty in the Not-for-Profit World

In the previous chapter, I highlighted the "golden rule" of marketing. This rule should be displayed in a prominent place on every desk of every person who engages in any form of marketing, and charities and universities are no exception.

People Renew the Way They Are Acquired

When someone graduates from college and becomes a lifetime prospect for annual giving, what resonates best with that person? The answer: a reminder of how her experiences during her years at that institution shaped her life—the professors she had, the campus she was at, her fellow students, the political and social events she lived through as an undergraduate or graduate student.

Indeed, those schools with the most successful fund-raising efforts almost always have a strong class agent program, where peers ask peers for that annual gift—not someone in the development office far removed from the experience shared by these classmates.

Charities are no different. People make a first-time gift because of a solicitation that strikes an emotional hot button—a homeless child saved, an endangered animal species that needs protection, a city soup kitchen that must expand, a symphony that wants to remain world class. Contributors will respond to future donation requests if they have a focus similar to the one that first got their response.

People donate for a specific reason to a specific appeal. The appeal can even be seasonal. A lot of folks make all their charitable contributions in December and at no other time. Some like to give monthly. Some don't.

Channels make a difference, too. Many folks 70 and over will give a donation or make a membership payment only through the mail. Younger Americans are comfortable doing everything online.

Whatever the specific hot button that drove that first-time contribution—it must absolutely be noted in the donor's computer file so that your institution keeps that "memory" of what triggered this first gift. The other critical piece of data is keeping track of consecutive years of giving. Reminding a donor that they gave X number of years in a row is the *single most powerful piece of news* you can convey to encourage them to keep giving year after year.

Not-for-profits have a second very important loyalty rule:

One Percent of the Contributors Give 50 Percent of the Money

I would wager a healthy sum that most nonprofits spend nowhere near 50 percent of their fund-raising resources on this 1 percent. Ironically, this elite group is a very manageable size, usually 500 to 5,000 people. Yet, most organizations do not really communicate properly with them and thus leave money on the table that otherwise might be turned into a significant donation.

Here are a few simple guidelines that will help in the care and cultivation of your most generous contributors:

- The top 1 percent generally gives at least 500 times more than the average donation to your organization. Whenever a donor reaches this level for the first time, the most senior official at your organization should call and thank him personally—without exception.
- All correspondence should be highly personalized. Do whatever you possibly can to make certain that top donors do not receive mass mailings and communications from your organization. A really nice touch is to send top donors advance copies of everything the rest of the donor base eventually receives. Be sure to tell them that they are receiving these items first—newsletters, alumni magazine, special group travel offers, and so on.

- Do not be concerned about overdoing continual communications with this top group. They are invested and want to feel part of the inner circle. The more you talk to them, the happier and more committed they will feel. Believe me, they will not be irritated by the attention. They want to hear from you. Just be sure to always add the personal touch.

- They should receive a personal letter from the most senior official from your organization every other month. The communication should be centered around a "state of the ship" report as well as information about upcoming special events they might want to attend—well in advance of the actual dates.

- If you have a campus environment, invite them to come speak on their life and career. Profile these people in your newsletters and magazines. Schools rarely profile their most successful business alumni, opting instead for teachers, social workers, and other alumni with various pet social causes. This approach is fine in moderation but not to the exclusion of showcasing successful businesspeople. After all, capitalism is what keeps those Ivy doors open!

- At universities, what I call "era merchandising" can be important and is generally ignored. Not just for your top donors, but for all donors, offer mugs, jackets, hats, blankets, chairs—from their era, not the present. They will be happy to buy, and you will make more money for your institution.

- Of course, always ask for feedback. A special e-mail address should be set up for the best donors to send in ideas, comments, complaints, and additional contributions. Institute a system to answer any and all of their e-mails within 48 hours. These people are important. Make sure they feel that way.

It is a thrill to be around people who love your organization and have the means to support it at a level way above the average contributor. The more time you devote to this group, the more successful your college or charity will be. An occasional phone call from your president or equivalent—at least once a year—is my final suggestion. Nothing beats individual recognition.

CHAPTER 12

THE SINGLE MOST POWERFUL WAY TO GET CUSTOMERS TO LOVE YOU

The simple fact is that the most powerful piece of data about your customers is also the most overlooked and underutilized: how many consecutive years they have been an active customer of yours. It is a hard fact of human evolution that we like to be part of a larger unit than ourselves. In fact, we must be to survive and prosper. The basic unit we all relate to is our immediate family, but we extend out far beyond family to all manner of "membership families" in the form of clubs, fraternal orders, sports teams, work teams, universities, charitable groups, and customer affliations.

The good news is that many businesses acknowledge they should recognize their customer's longevity. The bad news is that they do not have a clue how to really leverage this information. Take American Express, which is considered to be a consummate customer-focused enterprise and in many ways they excel at just that activity. Since the very beginning of their card business in 1958, they have listed on every card: member since _____. For the past decade or so, promotional letters from Amex are always finished with the executive's title below their name and then the line: Member

Since (with the date filled in). What American Express does not do, however, is list the cardmember's "member since" date within the same letter. That lack of recognition is a mistake. Millions of Amex's cardmembers view their consecutive years of membership as a visible status of their credit worth over time.

What American Express should be doing is to recognize the cardmember's years of membership at every opportunity and at every touch point—in promotional and service letters, on their web sites when a cardmember logs on, visible on the monthly billing statement, in e-mail communications, and in the form of a verbal thank you from Amex phone reps whenever a cardmember calls a service center.

Cardmembers who have been so for 5, 10, 15, and more years should have special promotions directed to them. Why? Because we all want to be recognized for our exceptional loyalty. We want to see it in black and white, and we feel better knowing that the business we have been loyal to makes the effort to remind us they know. Plus, what does it cost American Express to make this gesture? Zero. There is no incremental cost whatsoever.

The next example is about a related form of recognizing loyalty, and the company in question also is American—American Airlines. In 2007, I received a personalized letter along with luggage tags announcing I was now designated a Million Miler. A staggering accomplishment, to be sure, and I immediately thought of the millions of peanuts I consumed along the way. A nice benefit was mentioned—that from now on I would be upgraded automatically to first class from coach when space was available 48 hours before departure. Very classy. I felt great. And that was the end of the recognition.

Since the letter arrived five years ago I have never seen my Million Miler status mentioned anywhere else. Not on American's web site, not in subsequent correspondence, not even shown on my electronic ticket. What a total opportunity lost to continually reinforce my years of loyalty every time I interact with the airline. Moreover, if I see this status regularly, I would proudly tell friends and family of the extra effort American takes to recognize its long-time customers, implying they should "hop aboard" at every opportunity.

The amazing thing is that American has many thousands of loyal customers, as do all the airlines, who individually have flown millions of miles, and, like my personal example, never receive any recognition whatsoever. No special offers, no mileage total front and center when the customer logs on to the airline web site. It is, in a word, incomprehensible that no recognition is offered.

I have a friend of almost 40 years who dwarfs my mile-age accomplishment with American with a staggering total of 19 million miles flown to date. We laugh about the fact that American has never once made any effort to thank him for his business. Heck, at that level the CEO should call my pal annually just to say thank you. If he did, my friend would tell everyone he knows and the goodwill would spread to many of his traveling colleagues and friends. Such a simple thing to do. American doesn't do it, but you should with any uber customers you happen to have who outdistance all others with their level of purchase over time.

My last example of a missed opportunity in recognizing years of loyalty is in publishing—the *Wall Street Journal.*

Prior to Mr. Murdock's purchasing Dow Jones and the *Wall Street Journal,* I was an acquaintance of both the chief operating officer and the CEO. Fine gentlemen both, and several times a year they bought me lunch just to brainstorm on ways to increase subscriber loyalty. On one occasion I asked them if they knew how many subscribers had been doing so for 50 years or more. I was impressed that they knew the answer—approximately 50,000 readers out of 2.2 million. When I asked the question, I was thinking of my dad, who had been subscribing for nearly 60 years.

Here was a perfect opportunity to generate goodwill and good press. My suggestion was to hold a news conference and announce that every reader who passed the 50-year mark would get a framed copy of the front page from January 1 of the year they first subscribed. And after 50 years, they would only pay $50 a year to keep receiving the *Journal*—a substantial discount, but hey, they earned it.

An additional suggestion was to print occasional profiles of readers who had passed the 50-year subscriber milestone. It is a good bet a lot of unique stories would come to light and be compelling human-interest pieces. My friends at the top did not carry out these suggestions, so Mr. Murdock—there is still time.

One suggestion they did implement was to begin putting pictures of reporters and columnists adjacent to their articles. A nice touch and a way of making the *Journal* seem more human and less remote. After all, we relate to other people when we see them, and seeing the article author's picture makes us feel like they are speaking directly to us. Book publishers have been showing their authors on book jackets for a century. The *Journal* could take this technique one step further and add under the picture and their name the number of years they have written for the *Journal*.

My point is simple. Practically every company of every size stores data on the consecutive years a person has been a customer. And yet, as I mentioned earlier, virtually no company uses this data to continually reinforce why the customer should keep buying in the future.

You can really get a leg up on your competitors by reminding customers (or contributors if you run a non-profit group) at every opportunity that you appreciate their X years of consecutive purchasing with you.

Getting Your Promotional Letter Read or E-Mail Every Time

It's really as simple as starting the first sentence with the number of years a customer has been one. And build on that connection. Example:

Dear Mr. Smith:

Eighteen years have passed since you first opened an account with us at AnyBank USA. We are honored to be serving you for nearly two decades and want to always bring you the best service and offerings we can. That's why I am excited about a brand new product we have designed for you and our other long-term customers. (And so on. . . .)

The Absolute Power of Membership . . . and Something American Express Does Right

The American Express card was first introduced in 1958. When I worked at the firm from 1987 through 1991, we instituted a policy that never questions how long a customer thinks he has been a cardholder. I remember one day receiving an urgent call from a customer service senior executive. An elderly charter cardholder from 1958 had called to complain that his new replacement card had just arrived and incorrectly showed his membership as since 1958 when he knew he had been a member since 1956. "What should the customer service folks do?" I was asked. This wasn't the first time a customer had called to complain that he was right about his years of membership when, actually, he was wrong.

My response was simple. In this case, the customer is always right. If he thinks he has been a member since 1956, send him a card showing "member since 1956," even though no Amex card existed then. And we should be thrilled that customers care this much about their consecutive years of loyalty—real or imagined.

CHAPTER 13

MAKING SENSE OF MEDIA PLANNING

So much for the "good old days" repeated for three TV seasons now by the *Mad Men* series. Back then, media planning consisted of scoping out a handful of TV networks, a manageable number of magazines, some radio options, and billboards. And major advertisers during that era were prone to sponsor entire shows, which is simply unaffordable today for the most part.

The knee-jerk reaction for many advertisers now is to rush online and buy everything in sight. I would suggest pausing before doing that. There is a lot of research that makes it quite clear that you stand a better chance having your audience find you on TV than online. On a pure mathematical basis, there is no contest. It is well documented that we humans can only handle so much choice. The phrase "less is more" has always been one that marketers forget at their peril. In any event, here are a few numbers to keep in the back of your mind as you decide how best to find an audience for your product or service.

TV: There are roughly 500 channels, though millions of homes have access to far fewer. Most Americans favor on average 11 of these channels.

Radio: In any given metro area there are 40 to 60 stations, and 4 or 5 are popular on an individual basis.

Web sites: Best guess, about 50 million publicly accessible sites. Average number bookmarked is 11.

Also, the time involved daily in each channel may surprise you. The Internet ranks third. TV viewership by adult consumers averages 8 hours a day, radio 2.5 hours, and the Internet about 40 minutes of work-related activity.

All this activity adds up to the conclusion that you have the best chance of reaching a prospective customer on TV, followed by radio, and far behind these two—on your web site. Of course, there is paid search and advertising on currently popular web sites. Not crazy ideas and worth testing. Just remember that web site ad clutter long ago surpassed radio and TV, and it is just very hard to stand out in digital ad land. How you can will be discussed later.

Media planners throw around lots of acronyms, like CPM (cost per thousand) and GRP (gross rating points), that relate to the cost of reaching people through various media: print, TV, radio, Internet. But these terms and a bunch more have no bearing on whether the target audience actually sees your ad, enjoys it, and does something in response.

There are a lot of factors, some in your control and many not, that influence whether an ad campaign gets noticed by the right individuals and contributes to the success of the product or service that is advertised. Three of the most critical factors are ones you can control.

1. *Visual impact.* The ad or series of ads should be visually compelling and demand attention from the viewer or reader.
2. *Location.* You pay for the very best "real estate." You'll need that space in the magazine, or spot on TV, radio, or Internet that will most likely be seen or heard by the maximum number of people who fit your target profile.

3. *Frequency.* Within your budget, you should strive to maximize the number of times an ad appears.

Despite all the graphs and charts and mind-numbing numbers that media experts throw at you, these are the three factors that really count.

Much of this book is devoted to the number one factor, the creation of a compelling ad. The rest of this chapter will focus on the simple rules I follow to maximize media dollars through optimal placement and ad frequency.

There is no doubt that media planners at ad agencies or specialized media placement firms are a dedicated bunch who really thrive on their specialized craft. But they have a tendency to spread your media budget among as many media outlets as possible—broad reach, as they call it. You have another goal, which is much more critical to getting noticed. As I mentioned earlier, it's called *frequency.*

Are you better off having an ad appear a few times over a year in 30 magazines and newspapers or very frequently in 10? Same with radio stations and Internet sites—a few ads on many, or a lot on a few? The effect of frequency trumps occasional placements every time, even if you appear more frequently in fewer media vehicles.

Hand in hand with frequency is prime location. The only way to ensure that most readers see your ad is to pay for premium positioning whenever you can. None of us have unlimited budgets. In fact, usually we have fewer dollars to work with than we want. The best use of these dollars is to narrow down your media choices and pay the extra dollars required to buy premium space—the space that every reader is most likely to see.

Where might that be? Here are some tips.

Print Media

- *Magazines.* Top spots for readership are back cover, inside front cover, inside back cover, across from the table of contents, and opposite popular sections in the publication.

- *Newspapers.* The number one spot is page three, first section. Back page, first section is right up there. After that, it depends on the layout of the newspaper, what section makes sense for your product or service, and what section offers fewer ads from the competition.

In order to secure these top spots, you have to pay over and above normal rates. Prime real estate is all about location: a house on the beach costs more than a larger house a block inland. Same with media. Why pay any amount of money for a space somewhere in the publication that the vast majority of readers will either skim over or never see? Let the other guys do that.

Woody Allen once said, "Eighty percent of life is just showing up." Ad placement is a little trickier. It must be where most readers go instinctively, where they are likely to go every time they pick the publication in question or go to their favorite Internet site or TV show.

Most print media planning is not mysterious. You need to decide who your target audience is, what their media habits are likely to be, and determine the most visible locations in the publication. Then buy those spots as often as possible.

Take private banking. I ran marketing for various private banks as part of my overall marketing duties at four financial services firms. Hands down the absolute best ad placement is the inside front cover of *The Economist.*

Do you have a high-quality product or service targeted to women from 20 to 40? You can't beat the Sunday *New York Times* marriage announcement section.

Sticking with the Sunday *Times,* several advertisers swear by the magazine section—most notably the Bose Corporation, Mt. Sinai Hospital in New York City, and Rosetta Stone foreign language courses.

Zig When Everyone Else Zags

Bose is a great example of this strategy. They are a maker of high-quality moderately priced sound equipment. Their core audience fits precisely with the profile of the *Times* magazine reader—thoughtful, well-educated, and not scared off by an ad that goes into a bit of technical detail. Rather than advertise in magazines targeted to audio enthusiasts, which are jam-packed with sound equipment ads, Bose goes where all their competitors do not: the Sunday *Times* magazine. They figured out that getting noticed means not being one of many choices, but being the *only* choice in a publication in their category.

Mt. Sinai and Rosetta Stone have similar strategies. Mt. Sinai is positioning itself as the hospital for intelligent people to rely on (who also tend to have great health insurance), and Rosetta is a very expensive approach to interactive foreign language learning—which appeals to the intellectual crowd.

Women's fashion advertising is another case in point. Pick up any issue of *Vanity Fair* magazine, that is, if you are strong enough to lift it. There are so many fashion ads, page after page after page, that the feature articles seem almost like afterthoughts. Will any one ad get noticed? Not likely.

All financial services companies want to advertise in the same business sections of newspapers or business-oriented magazines, and their ads are usually densely cluttered in those pages. But what about newspaper sections or nonbusiness publications less populated by competitors, like sports, automotive, or arts and lesiure. You have a much better chance of standing out. It is just that simple.

TV and Radio Placement

The same rules for print media apply to these two options: excite the viewer or listener with your message, be in the most visible spot possible, and be there as much as possible.

Ads are annoying on TV. They do allow bathroom breaks, but still no one likes these constant interruptions. The one big exception to this rule is the Super Bowl, where the ads have become a game unto themselves and often spark more discussion the day after than the football outcome.

But whether you place an ad on a 2 A.M. late show or reruns of *Murder, She Wrote,* or plunk down $3 million for a Super Bowl spot, the most desirable position is the first ad spot in the first commercial break. You are far better off having one ad every week for a year in the first commercial break of a weekly show than multiple ads for a few months in the same show. Like a magazine's inside front cover, this position is where the largest number of viewers is likely to notice the ad. And like a magazine, where readership drops off the further into the magazine you go, TV ad viewership drops off 95 percent of the time after the first commercial break. Depending on the show, it may not drop significantly, but it is still extremely rare for ad viewership to increase as a show progresses.

For a number of years now, the biggest threat to TV advertising is TiVO or its DVR equivalent. Ongoing studies of consumer TV habits compiled by Forrester Research point out that when people watch prerecorded shows they skip 92 percent of the commercials. Not good news for advertisers or the commercial TV industry.

And DVR usage is widespread today, with about 30 percent of households so equipped. During this decade, DVR capability will likely grow to 60 or 70 percent of American homes. Where does this leave viewership of the TV spot you spend all that time and money to produce?

You Can Avoid Consumer Ad Skipping

The best defense against ad skipping will continue to be advertising on shows that are least likely to be recorded for later viewing. The two categories that lead the pack are news and sports. It's also reaffirmed in research that 93 to 95 percent of viewers with delayed viewing options continue to watch local news in real time. After all, the morning weather report doesn't do you much good the next day. Following local news in real-time popularity is national news, sports events, and special events like the Oscars or Emmys.

Clearly, news and sports shows will become more desirable to TV advertisers in the years ahead. In addition, television producers will try and combat ad skipping with more real-time interactive events for viewers to participate in during scheduled programming.

The Next Giant Leap in Ad Watching

Another way to encourage consumers to watch ads is coming on strong over the next few years through major efforts by the cable giants to direct targeted TV ads to each household. At one level this is the simple application of massive data processing power specifically applied to analyze program viewing habits at the household level. The data originates through the cable box and allows advertisers to cash in on targeting messages on specific shows that are being watched. Telling viewers the ads are just for them should boost interest—especially since special deals can be offered for each household based on what they are watching, taking into account other data the cable companies can acquire on the occupants of each household. And that data is considerable. Data like age, income level, occupation, children at home and their ages, and on and on.

Here's an example: Judy and Jack Miller have two children, ages 8 and 10. One frequently watched show is CBS's *Hawaii Five-O*. Accordingly, Hyatt Hotels delivers an ad during the show with an offer for a family vacation for the Millers to Hawaii. Far-fetched? Not at all. This personalized ad approach will ultimately be the way most TV advertising is delivered.

Has Radio Seen Its Best Days?

Not at all. Radio is still a great medium. You can buy local markets very easily, and the cost to produce radio spots is peanuts compared to TV. There is no DVR to worry about—radio is 100 percent real time, and ad placement is pretty simple—drive time. Prime radio is 6:00 to 8:30 A.M. and 4:00 to 7:30 P.M. Radio is overlooked by a lot of marketers, and it shouldn't be. Radio is great for small businesses and not-for-profit organizations that want to reach a broad audience and just cannot afford TV.

Commuting by car will continue for decades, for sure, and there are more cars on the road every year. You should take advantage of this fact and seriously consider radio as part of most marketing campaigns. Sound by itself in many ways is more powerful than the sight that TV adds to the equation. With just sound, your mind works harder and imagines what it wants to. That can work in an advertiser's favor.

The Internet

There is good news and there is bad. First, the good news: Internet advertising can be highly targeted because audience segmentation is a given. For instance, people who frequent NBA.com love pro basketball. Advertisers of different stripes, such as beer, pizza, Ticketmaster, and so on, can zero in and make pitches that complement the online programming. Travel sites are great places to offer hotel and resort deals, car rental options, and leisure clothing. On the major news sites the financial services providers are always out in full force, as are the high-end car manufacturers.

The other good thing about Internet advertising is that often, as an advertiser, you pay only for people who click on your ad, at which point it's up to you to wow them to become customers or qualified prospects.

So what's the problem? The problem is that a lot of clicks don't always translate into conversions. Web advertising typically has two problems: (1) the sound and visuals are inferior to the power of sound on radio and the compelling

Internet Advertising that Excites and Delights

In my role as Executive Vice President of AARP, we recently hired Betty White to "put a face on the place" and to do so with some edginess that AARP has not attempted in the past. Among multiple uses of Betty in different media, we created an online enrollment ad that includes a video welcome from Betty if you click on the ad. Seeing Betty as the focal point of the ad with a very pointed headline, as in: "You are now 50 or older—Get Over It," will draw folks in, in spite of themselves, and will make them smile and consider more fully membership in AARP. Find "your Betty" and see how response will dramatically improve over just words on a Web page accompanied by numbing stock photography.

nature of television as a medium that draws attention visually and verbally like no other medium can, and (2) Internet advertising can be quite impersonal. There is no human speaking in the vast majority of ads. Print also has that problem, of course, but consumers don't have high interactive expectations for print. They do for the Web.

My advice, therefore, is to think about having a spokesperson of some sort as the focal point of your Internet advertising. Think of your ad as a TV ad on the Web, and take it from there. And like in a well—conceived direct-response TV ad, you should have a strong call to action that includes giving the consumer the option of calling you. I am struck by how many Internet advertisers forget that millions of consumers still want to call in orders—this is particularly true of clothing, big-ticket items in general, and business-to-business services.

Global Media Planning and Placement

Global media planning is still a challenge, since the popularity of media channels by country can vary widely, and translation from English to other languages is often poorly done despite the best intentions of translators.

So what are some of the specific regional challenges to media buying outside the United States? Latin America is an extremely difficult region to plan ad campaigns. Though mostly Spanish speaking, the nuances in Spanish can vary quite a bit from country to country. Plus, TV viewership is hard to pin down, and there are few magazines that have any significant circulation, especially business publications. What's more, direct mail is unreliable and costly. Africa is even more difficult. In the more developed countries around the world, TV is king and Internet advertising is increasing by leaps and bounds. Daily newspapers are also still strong in many countries in Europe and Asia. It may surprise you to know that in the United States and worldwide, based on a 2010 PricewaterhouseCoopers study, newspapers handily beat Internet and mobile in total ad dollars spent.

In terms of creativity, there are country-specific issues, but most are manageable. As a rule, a global marketing campaign should have the same look and feel in every country where the product or service is being offered. The basic sales message is often pretty much the same, although local language will dictate different slants to make the same point.

Often, you run across tactical issues such as whether to include English in part of an ad that is in a different local language. In Japan, for instance, headlines and punch lines are often in English. English is viewed as hip and cool when used in these two ways.

In some Arabic-speaking countries, the locals like their ads in Arabic but prefer the call to action in English or in both languages.

When you go global, an agency's worth really gets tested. Insist on working with an ad agency with solid global experience. Fortunately, most agencies today are part of a global network, with experts in each region of the world. Your U.S.-based team should be able to tap into that local expertise and present you with a coherent and comprehensive plan for whatever product you want to promote in multiple countries.

CHAPTER 14

MAKING SOCIAL NETWORKING WORK FOR YOU

A really brief history: Passing a story or a point of view from one person to another or many others has been going on for well over 10,000 years. The only difference between our ancestors and us is that they communicated in order to survive day to day and we social network to give our opinion to anybody and everybody willing to listen. And technology makes communicating instantly with whomever wants to see our opinion a part of the fabric of modern culture. Said another way—Facebook, Twitter, blogs, and the like are here to stay and will remain a force in human expression and social change for the rest of human existence.

What drives people to become self-proclaimed experts on the Web is simply that we want to feel like we can make a difference and we want others to value our opinion. We are the ultimate social animals. Left alone, really alone, we go stark raving mad. We need social interaction to remain balanced and happy, and the Internet allows us this opportunity every second of every day from a variety of devices. In fact, it's interesting to note that the one modern technical convenience that is falling behind in relevance is the everyday, ordinary phone call. I can predict with some clarity that the simple act of one person calling another is going the way of the personal letter. It will continue to happen, but less and less often.

Texting, instant messaging, SMS, blogging, tweeting, and so on are ways the global village operates increasingly over time. How can your company get into this digital free-for-all and get a piece of the action?

In a sense, the answer is so simple that you will nod your head and say, "of course." But execution is always harder. What drives consumers worldwide to pay attention to one thing or another is, in a word—*news*. We crave the latest news, and unlike in all of human history through most of the 20th century, now we can publicly comment on news to all who digitally stumble upon our opinion.

The "secret" to an effective social networking strategy is new and fresh content to talk about as often as possible and get others to talk about. The same selling principles apply to networking socially as selling in any other form—create excitement however you can. Examples: brand new, never before offered, or limited quantity, so order ASAP; or here's an advance look before the general public; and so on.

You can read endless articles and a mountain of books on social networking, but it's not that complicated. You need a solid network of family and friends and, if possible, customers and a pacing strategy (more on that later).

Some Helpful Hints to Capitalize on Social Networking

These are not in order of importance. They are all good to remember.

- Create a Facebook account and build contact strategy around customer preferences for new or existing products and breaking news about your company. It's a great channel to launch products and test inexpensively.

- You never need to do traditional focus groups again. Save a small fortune—social networking is *much* faster, cheaper, and statistically valid.
- LinkedIn is the ultimate job network site. Good place to promote related products and services. Great place to find job candidates. Why pay headhunters ever again?
- Twitter—fast and furious growth pace. In a sense, just shorthand blogging. Mixed opinions on advertising effectiveness. Try it and find out.
- Craigslist has one-upped eBay. Tremendous amount of useful information well organized. Not cheap to advertise broadly but can be tested locally.
- Fastest-growing segment of participants are women 55 and older. And Baby Boomers (born 1947 to 1964) network more than any other age group.

Financial Considerations

- Social network sites are great spots to test advertising your service or product and generally you can arrange to pay per lead or order. And unlike conventional advertising you get feedback very quickly—often in hours.
- It is good to have five top metrics that you can measure—in particular traffic to your web site, from where, plus most popular pages, numbers and type of leads, and what is being bought.
- Advertising on these sites can produce a return on investment at least five times more profitable than traditional lead sources. The question is whether you are getting the volume you need.
- Assuming you have an annual marketing budget over $1 million, devote 10 percent to "playing in this space," that is, learning, and being nimble enough to ramp up quickly if results dictate.

Questions I Am Asked about the Future Direction of Media

Q: Will traditional media eventually disappear as social networking takes over?

A: No, certain magazines, such as fashion focused, will remain popular for many years to come. Outdoor media will remain popular as long as there are cars! TV is alive and well, and viewership continues to expand.

Q: Is clutter a potential issue that social networking will suffer from?

A: Yes. Like any other medium, there is too much messaging and too little time for most consumers to digest it all.

Q: Are any offline businesses able to benefit from the continual growth of online chatter and online buying?

A: For sure the shipping industry, most notably UPS and FedEx. Their combined growth is estimated at $100 billion in 2012, up from $30 billion in 2007 and $5 billion in 2001. The travel industry also benefits greatly from not needing travel agents cutting into their margins. Even politicians and charities are way better off collecting donations online and avoiding more expensive direct mail whenever possible.

Q: What is the number one challenge to building a popular web site that will get everyone in my target market to pay attention?

A: Fresh, compelling content.

Q: Will networking ever slow down and even shrink in popularity?

A: It is possible that many consumers will simply wear themselves out and admit to being overwhelmed. Effect would be to reduce the circle of folks they talk to and respond to. There is even a term for less networking: *pruning*.

Now from pruning to pacing. . . .

Pacing Is Important

One thing no one ever mentions on the subject of social networking is how often you should "send the word out." The best advice I can give is: do so when there is something of significance to communicate. In that way, folks will know that when you appear in their digital community, it's worth taking note. A constant stream of messaging works only for a few information addicts. The rest of us need space between hearing about company-product-service news—unless we proactively seek it out. That's just as true with regard to the use of e-mail addresses supplied by prospects and customers. Many companies send e-mails to their house list promoting one thing or another nearly every day and sometimes multiple times per day. This approach is dead wrong. It is annoying and counterproductive to keeping a customer happy. E-mail is actually more disruptive than direct mail. At least with direct mail, it all gets delivered at the same time six days a week. And you pick it up from your mailbox when you want to. E-mail arriving often buzzes or vibrates Blackberries and iPhones, and unwanted e-mail can crowd out messages that really should be read.

It is not a big surprise that on average companies have only 18 to 20 percent of their customers' e-mail addresses. Consumers fear overcommuncation via e-mail, and many won't give their address out; to a large degree, they are right.

Chat Rooms and Blogging

One might begin by asking who has the time to chitchat all day long and comment endlessly on what a particular company is doing well or not so well. Like beer drinkers in America, where a very small percentage drink most of the beer, probably several million Americans out of 310 million are active participants on blog sites and related venues. If you run a midsize to large company, you should provide community chat rooms and blogging opportunities so that others don't do it for you and in ways often not flattering to your business. And remember, there are always a few nuts out there who want to complain about anything and everything. Sometimes the best response is no response. You have to be the judge.

Firms with solid blogging strategies include FedEx, Apple, Starbucks, and Best Buy. Check out what they do and see what you can "steal."

Texting, Messaging, and Mobile

Forget about texting and messaging for commercial purposes. For starters, it is not practical and this is not the way to endear yourself to customers of any age or mind-set. Mobile is another matter entirely. There are mobile apps for practically everything. Many are free; some are not. Your business should, if possible, offer mobile entry to your product or service. And by its very nature, when a consumer attaches to your mobile application, they are giving you permission to interact in this fashion.

The latest technique, which will only get more sophisticated and popular, is combining a global positioning system (GPS) with a mobile app. For instance, Zagat, the well-known restaurant rating service, allows its app users to indicate where they are at the moment in a city and receive instant information on restaurants nearby.

Stores with multiple locations can alert customers via mobile when they are physically near a location with a special sale on an item of possible interest given past purchase history. A prediction—online data services will one day soon alert two people who may be a good match that they are approaching each other on the sidewalks of Manhattan or other urban centers. Now that's the ultimate "bumping into each other."

There is no end in sight to the popularity of mobile phone applications. And every company of any size must find a way to participate. Ultimately, most payments at physical locations nationwide will be possible by using a mobile phone as a smart debit card. Already, airline boarding passes can be downloaded and scanned off the phone screen as the passenger boards. New uses will pop up at regular intervals. Certainly, the transfer of patient-to-doctor medical information will gain traction in the years ahead. Paper tickets of all types will be replaced by scanning your mobile screen. The mobile phone will increasingly be the one device that must be carried at all times and will be indispensable to daily life. In many ways, it already is.

CHAPTER 15

E-MAULED—HOW TO AVOID CONSUMER RAGE

I touched upon the title of this chapter in the previous one. There are a few rules of the road that I recommend so that you and your customer have a healthy e-mail relationship. Most firm don't have a strategy that is customer friendly, and that is why, sadly for marketers, so few consumers willingly provide their e-mail addresses to companies they do business with.

Steve's Three Tips to Better E-mail Interaction with Consumers

1. Tell all customers and prospects at every opportunity that your e-mail policy is simple—you do not sell their e-mail address to other companies or allow other companies to pitch your customers using the e-mail address the consumer gave you.
2. Tell all customers and prospects that they should go to your web site, register, and fill out a preference survey indicating what products and services you offer that they want to hear about and when. They

should also be asked how often they wish to receive e-mail announcements from you—daily, twice a week, weekly, monthly, or rarely.

3. Your outbound e-mail should always be signed by a real person from your company, and the recipient should be allowed to respond back. It is poor form to send an e-mail and not allow for a response.

And here are some questions I am frequently asked about the use of e-mail, and my advice back.

Q: What's the one thing you would tell someone they have to do above all else to ensure a successful e-mail campaign?

A: E-mail is not some magical medium that defies the basic rules of marketing. You must still have a solid offer and the best positioning possible of your product or service to ensure success. The good news is that there are easy, fast, and inexpensive ways to test your offer by e-mail before you launch a major campaign of any kind. Two excellent online research sister companies are Research Now and e-Miles, with literally millions of consumers who have volunteered to review product and service offerings and are used by thousands of marketers worldwide.

Q: What's the biggest mistake marketers are still making with e-mail marketing?

A: It's still too much of a one-way street. Real feedback is not encouraged. Companies send an offer or ask for an opinion (i.e., customer survey) and yet provide no means for the recipient to directly communicate back to them. All types of companies are sending frequent e-mail surveys. But rarely do they report back the results and almost never ask for additional comments that will be seen by a company employee and responded to quickly or at all. This goes for political office holders as well—it takes most weeks to answer an inbound e-mail. That's just plain unacceptable. Remember call centers? E-mail should be no different. E-mail is a very personal two-way communication—or should be. But most marketers fail to understand that *personal* means responding to the individual and not treating them as one of thousands or millions who happen to be on an e-mail list.

Q: Are any new formats emerging within e-mail marketing?

A: Yes—ties to social media. Many e-mails now encourage advocates to "post to social," allowing campaigns to spread virally. The one outcome to be sensitive to is that your message is also apt to spread to nontargeted individuals.

Q: What's the best way to avoid having your e-mail deleted immediately?

A: Brand yourself immediately on the "from" and "subject" lines. Seventy percent of consumers say the "from" line is how they base their decisions to open or ignore; 30 percent say the subject line. Not surprising—and just reinforces that you should make your brand equity work in those two spots or risk being ignored.

Q: Is there a way or specific language that can be used in the subject line that will almost ensure that your e-mail will be opened by the recipient?

A: It is all about announcing real news, such as "One-Day Sale," "Five days left to act," "Product Alert," "Daily News Flash," "Breaking News," "Your status has been upgraded," "You are invited," and so forth. E-mail is the perfect vehicle to announce what just happened *when* it happened. Always keep that in mind and you will be successful.

Q: E-mail marketing has been around for quite some time. Is it still effective, and how dramatically? Is it changing on a yearly basis?

A: Volumes have increased year to year for the past few years at roughly 15 percent. Consumers continue to spend more time online, and e-mail adoption and use continue to grow, including connections to social and mobile communications. Forrester Research predicts continued growth for the next 5 years at 11 percent annually. Contributing factors are more adoption by small businesses, the relentless and positive move to paperless communications, and easier navigation for online shopping. E-mail marketing provides terrific shopping and shipping values for millions of time-starved consumers who can't or won't brave the hassle of driving to malls and stand-alone stores with the added inconvenience of uneven inventories to choose from and lugging items home.

Q: What are some of the key things marketers look to, to use e-mail effectively?

A: Two words: *frequency* and *relevance*. You should always be testing whether it's the subject line, an offer, timeliness, or cadence. As mentioned earlier, e-Miles is a great test lab before a major campaign is launched, whether by e-mail only or incorporating multimedia. And marketers pay e-Miles only for those consumers who see the offer and answered a few relevant questions.

Q: What are the average response and open rates for e-mail marketing messages today?

A: Open rate—22 percent. Click rate—27 percent of opens, meaning a 5 percent response rate. These rates assume consumers are familiar with your company and have some prior connection. There are several techniques that can boost these averages. The most basic but often overlooked is a thank you e-mail arriving soon after a product or service purchase—incorporating an additional offer.

Q: If you were to group all marketers together using e-mail today, what percentage would you guesstimate have a clue as to how to use it effectively?

A: Twenty percent, given that we all believe the 20/80 rule. In this case, 20 percent of marketers really understand how to create effective, compelling e-mail campaigns. Yes, this percentage should be higher. One area that retards results is the lack of attention to cadence or frequency of e-mails. An example is online movie ticketing companies that send an e-mail survey a day after online tickets are bought. The survey is sent even if you have never responded over months or years, and the consumer is never asked in advance if she wants to receive the surveys. Annoying to those who just want to buy tickets online. And many other companies do exactly the same thing. It is imperative with every new e-mail customer that you ask up front what type of messages they want to get and when.

Q: Is e-mail losing its effectiveness with the growth of social media?

A: Not at all. Various studies suggest strong growth in volume for years to come. One reason is that e-mail is private meaning from one entity direct to the consumer. And back. Social media is the opposite of private. The vast majority of e-mail use folks don't want to share with others—from buying drugs to online dating to cars, managing finances, self-help aids, travel plans, and much more.

CHAPTER 16
WEB WASTED—DON'T YOU

Every company on the planet needs a web site, and most likely everyone has one or multiple sites in the 21st century. Therein lies the problem—how do you get noticed and get a steady flow of visits to your site?

The best answer I can give is that 98 percent of the time you should seek outside help to build and maintain your web site. Even very large companies often outsource the whole effort, much like these same companies outsource their computer processing to specialists like IBM Services.

Like the game of golf, it looks easy from afar. How difficult can it be to hit a ball on the ground that's not moving? How difficult can it be to organize and design a web site? To both questions, "damn difficult" is the answer.

And if you are a really small business, don't despair. There are equally small design firms that specialize in building web sites at a very reasonable cost. Through Google, you can find an abundance of these specialty shops and thus avoid going to major agencies where a small fortune is required to sign on the Internet design, build, and maintain team.

Based on my analysis of thousands of web sites over the past 10 years, most suffer from the same digital affliction. In no particular order:

- Way too much information is crammed onto the home page.
- All body type is far too small and, of course, sans serif, which is hard for the eye to adjust to and read.
- It is not clear to the visitor what to focus on or how to enroll.
- Who runs the place? There is no welcome on the home page from the CEO or owner, thus no warmth or personality—just product or service listings scattered about.
- Flash billboards change too quickly and just annoy rather than beacon involvement.
- The brand promise or tagline is completely missing.
- There is too much third-party advertising.
- There is no reason to return to the web site regularly.

The last bullet point above is perhaps the most important to take into consideration. After all, the whole point of a web site is to attract the maximum number of visitors around the clock. The more "eyeballs," the more potential business and the more potential for you to sell others on advertising on your site.

The way to build traffic is the same way TV shows build an audience—fresh content every day or week without fail. And that's just for staying in the game. To really be successful you should employ an offer engine that headlines special offers every day tailored to who is likely to be your customer. These can be price offers or add-on service offers or brand new items "hot off the press." Moreover, if a visitor makes a purchase when he returns to the site, even if it is seconds later, there should be a fresh new offer waiting.

And web sites should be visually compelling and fun for the eye to scan. Most are boring beyond belief and take themselves far too seriously—financial service sites being a prime example. One way to pump up the volume on a site is to have ongoing video clips of experts explaining the ins and outs of whatever business you are in.

What are some good sites to look at for inspiration? In financial services, Fidelity and Morgan Stanley. American Express also does a solid job. In other fields, Amazon, Best Buy, Zagat, American Airlines, Fresh Direct, and informational sites like *Fortune* magazine, *Esquire,* and, yes, *People.*

A really nifty site that is popular with newly minted lawyers is Bitter Lawyer. It is edgy to the extreme and a good lesson in how to involve and entertain every visitor from the first moment they arrive at the home page.

Another technique not in common use is to personalize the content by location. If a person lives in Fairfax, Virginia, she should see different content than someone in Atlanta, Georgia, assuming you sell and service on a national scale. But even if you do not, the more you can localize the content, the better. And don't forget to highlight upcoming events or webinars, podcasts, and the like.

Something No One Else Ever Does

Few sites take into account the ebb and flow of daily life. Consumers tend to be more relaxed later at night when the little ones are in bed, and on the weekends—particularly Sundays. You can take advantage of late night and Sundays by offering special content during those time periods, including contests, giveaways, product or service research polling, and even special guests on a video clip or podcast.

Another approach rarely employed is making it clear that certain areas of the web site are just for your most loyal customers and that special benefits await them and others who want to join their ranks.

The bottom line is that most web sites are painfully boring or too unfocused, along with lacking any personality or attitude that could get consumers to really enjoy the journey to your site and make it a regular stop.

Just follow the simple advice in this chapter and you can rise above the blah sites and be a real destination.

CHAPTER 17

NO ONE EVER BOUGHT ANYTHING FROM AN ENGLISH PROFESSOR

So do not write like one.

Think of the opening of a promotional letter or e-mail as a headline that needs to grab reluctant readers and draw them in—like the one-line paragraph that opens this chapter. To guarantee readership, a letter, unless it's from the IRS, needs short sentences; very short paragraphs, some just one sentence long; and a ton of white space, which is pleasing to the eye, much like a well-crafted brochure.

As I said in an earlier chapter, salutations get in the way. I suggest you leave them out unless you know the person's name or nickname for sure. "Dear Friend" is just plain dumb—I am not your friend and I don't know you. Dear Reader . . . Dear Colleague . . . Dear Employee—they all sound like you are addressing the "Dearly Beloved" leader of North Korea. And they all telegraph one message you should avoid: this is a form letter going to hundreds, thousands, or millions of people. Why remind your audience that they are one of so many? Immediately open with a headline and you are way ahead of all the other "Dear Friend" letters out there.

Those of us who write promotional letters for a living are routinely asked how long a letter should be for maximum impact. My answer is worthy of any politician's mushy response to a direct question: the letter should be only as long as is necessary to tell the story. Given current attention levels, my general advice is to stick to one-page letters most of the time. If a product has a lot of features and options, you can provide an attachment with the details and thus keep the actual letter as short as possible.

My all-time favorite example of "short can be way better than long" comes from the world of fund-raising, an industry where letter writing has been a core competency for decades. One of the most successful fund-raising letters ever written was three short sentences penned by a television evangelist facing a bigger-than-usual financial crisis in his ministry. He sent 2 million one-page letters to his database of previous contributors. Each letter simply read: "Major financial crisis. No time to explain now. Please send anything you can!" And they did.

Back to that short attention span, which can often work in your favor. No one remembers the content of a letter. Sure, you remember you received a letter asking for money or selling a subscription, but you rarely remember the actual wording. If you craft a promotional letter that really works, you can use it with very little modification over and over and over again.

Years ago, my colleague John Groman, a world-class direct-marketing dynamo, wrote a fund-raising letter for the Boston Symphony. The letter was so effective that the symphony used the exact same letter for five years in a row to kick off their annual fund-raising campaign. The only thing that changed was the date. Each year, the letter was mailed to about 50,000 followers of the symphony. The symphony never received a single phone call or letter asking why they sent the exact same letter each year. Instead, all they received were record-level donations.

In the commercial world, the *Wall Street Journal* has used the same subscription prospecting letter for close to 25 years. Sure, professional letter writers notice (all three of us), but no one else does or cares.

If you happen on a promotional letter that gets great response from your customers and/or prospects, let them get excited all over again next year and the year after that.

Another technique to use with e-mail or direct mail is what I call the *one-two punch*. Send a very short letter to your target audience telling them that they will receive a special mailing with an exciting offer, just for them, in a couple of days. Of course, the follow up e-mail or mailing must come across as a unique or valuable offer. I have seen this one-two strategy work for any kind of business or not-for-profit group many times. The more loyal the customer group is to your product or service, the better this technique will work.

A variation of this technique is to send a letter notifying the recipients that their response is required right away or you will follow up the letter with a phone call. If done properly in the right tone, you can dramatically boost response by "threatening" to call them.

We Are Wired as a Species to Say Yes!

For sure, you never learned this fact in English Literature class and probably not in Psychology 101 either.

Humans hate to say the word *no*. In some cultures, most notably Japanese, people go to great lengths to avoid saying no to anyone at any time, even though that's the message they would like to deliver.

You can take advantage of this hardwiring of our universal gene pool if you always structure a customer offer with a yes/no option. Not-for-profit organizations were the first groups to use this technique widely. For many years now, it seems to have disappeared from most offers, and that is a mistake.

Here is a hypothetical example of a yes/no option for the Fresh Air Fund, one of my favorite charities.

Check one and return this reply card:

____Yes, I want to contribute $____ to help send inner-city kids to summer camp to give them an experience that will last a lifetime.

____No, I don't wants kids to have the experience of a few weeks of summer in the country away from the heat-baked sidewalks and streets of New York.

I think you get the point.

CHAPTER 18

LEVERAGING BOOMER POWER AND MORE

The facts are pretty clear. There are roughly 100 million consumers age 50 and above, and they control the vast majority of assets and disposable dollars in America.

And we are getting "older by the minute." For the next 10 years, 7,000 to 10,000 Baby Boomers a day will be turning 65. This march toward old age, despite Boomers' never wanting to admit to it, has not been lost on advertisers. Media buyers are demanding more programming tailored to mature audiences, and Hollywood is attempting to churn out films that will draw intergenerational audiences and are appropriate for Boomers and their grandchildren.

Boomers (folks born between 1945 and 1965) number roughly 80 million and are the first generation in history to live much longer than all who preceded them. Social upheaval has been a steady occurrence. Boomers grew up during the "golden era of TV" and still watch more of it than any other age group. They grew up with Woody Woodpecker and grew into Woodstock, Vietnam, the Pill, AIDS, equality in the workforce, and record amounts of interfaith and interracial marriage . . . and divorce.

Recent surveys of Boomers indicate they are generally happy with their lives, which in some ways is surprising given, unlike previous generations, they did not follow the traditional happiness path of college–marriage–kids–one company for life–pension–move to Florida. In fact, over 90 percent say they plan on living the rest of their lives in the same community and, if possible, the same house.

There are dark clouds. They have saved very little, and their primary asset, their home, has lost a lot of value over the past few years and a housing recovery in full force may never happen again. They are also not particularly healthy, and one in three is obese by medical standards. How they will affect the economy in the next few decades and how marketers should target them is an ongoing debate with many predictions. My own are below.

As the Boomers age, the rest of the world is right there with us. In fact, the populations of Europe and Asia are aging faster than those of the United States and most Third World countries. By 2020, one-half of the population of Europe, including Russia, will be 50 or older, and Japan will top all other nations with the oldest average age.

Conventional wisdom, which often isn't so wise, has it that as populations age, they tend to consume less. They drive less often. They don't buy as much new clothing. They don't need the latest computer or mobile gadget. What's more, they downsize their housing needs and consume less food, soda, and alcohol.

The real story is that there will be winners and losers in the marketplace as America and most of the rest of the world grows older and older. Here are some predictions that marketers should pay attention to:

- Older Americans are done moving. They want to stay in their homes and remain part of their communities. This "I am planted for good" attitude bodes well for home improvement products and services. The downside is that new home building will slow eventually to a level never seen before. And I sense that the softness in the housing market is here to stay.

- Health care services today are roughly 17 percent of total gross national product (GNP). That number is going in one direction in the years ahead—up. Worldwide, the medical community will have more business than it can handle, and rationed health care will become a reality for many.
- The political issues surrounding health care, the related topic of caregiving, and Social Security will become ever more important in winning elections and managing the U.S. and global economy.
- Content providers—particularly all forms of TV and digital entertainment—should have a bright future.
- Certain leisure industries will be in greater demand, such as professional sports and fitness clubs catering to the 50-plus crowd.
- After many years of virtually no growth, golf may see an "upswing" as record numbers of men retire over the next 20 years.
- Fast food will potentially gain in popularity and be less fast, with more pleasant seating and expanded menus.
- With record numbers of single older Americans predicted for the next three decades, expenditures on pet care (for their four-legged companions) and related services will keep rising from the current $47 billion a year to God knows what—a much larger number for sure.

All these predictions will happen in one way or another. How severely remains to be seen. As I said in my first book in 2005, this shift to older worldwide hasn't happened before to this degree. Future marketing strategies will have to be more aligned with what the 50-to-70 crowd find relevant to enjoying their time left on the planet.

Eight Other Predictions Marketers Can Count On

1. In the 21st century, there are two basic consumer categories: adults and little adults. Maturation seems to happen at warp speed. Young children want to do the same things adults do—they want to surf the Net at age three. They want and get mobile phones and texting features and enter the adult digital world from birth, beginning and possibly ending 90 years later on Facebook. They are completely immersed in the adult world and watch more of our programs, eat the same food, and travel farther and more frequently than previous younger generations.

2. Leisure travel will be more and more popular and increasingly intergenerational. Resorts will need to relate to all ages, with more focus than ever before. And the presence of pets on vacation will increase dramatically.

3. Safety, security, reliability, ease of use. These are the four big product features that consumers will base many of their buying decisions on. The products that shine in these areas will win.

4. The number one nonwork activity after sleep will remain TV viewing. Even though TV seems like a dated term, the flat screen on the wall will continue to be our "electronic fireplace" and the hours spent watching some form of programming, including interactive participation and personalized ad pitches, will increase year after year. Pundits have predicted the demise of the networks for decades. They are wrong. Cable is a huge success, and guess who owns most of the cable stations—the networks. The biggest challenge to the entire entertainment industry will be to provide enough programming to meet the demand.

5. More Americans will be single than ever before, either by choice or as the remaining spouse. As a result, online dating services appear to have a bright

future. Also, our basic animal companions, dogs and cats, will be more a part of our daily lives than ever before. The companion dog industry, such as demand for seeing-eye dogs, will rise. Pet sitting will become a significant source of extra income for many seniors.

6. Quality in all forms will reign supreme. It always has been the big mama of product marketing and is often the one determinant for ensuring success. When you ship a package via FedEx, you expect 100 percent reliability that your package will arrive as promised. In the early years of FedEx, you expected this reliability but had no access to the status along the way to ultimate delivery. Today, the quality of information on the location of the package is as important as the physical movement. Even the pizza industry has taken note. Domino's allows customers online to follow the making of and ultimate delivery of their pizza on a minute-by-minute basis.

7. Consumers will increasingly demand quality products that last. This is not a new trend; it just continues. In the case of the food industry, this means fussier buyers of frozen and fresh food items. Our indispensable mobile devices will have to be smarter and easier to use, with networks that are more reliable. We all may live to see cars essentially driving themselves from one destination to the other—like planes have done for years. At some not-too-distant point in the future, a 90-year-old with poor eyesight will be able to "drive" just as well as a 32-year-old with perfect vision. The car will do 100 percent of the driving.

8. Highly personalized direct mail may make a comeback, assuming the Post Office doesn't price itself out of business. Older Americans will have more time to read whatever mail they receive and may even look forward to it. Plus, catalogs will remain popular. The Web just can't replace the fun of flipping through colorful fun pages of fashion items and home wares.

Surprisingly, there are far fewer generational gaps than ever before. Even in categories most prone to gap behavior, such as movies, music, and fashion, there is a merging of tastes not evident in past decades. Baby Boomers want to look as young as possible, and their kids try to look like younger versions of the parents. Music tastes seems to be a shared activity, and family units still exist. Shared values remain.

The troubling gap that will persist in the years ahead will be between the dwindling number of young people and the larger number of older ones who depend on social programs funded by taxing the younger workforce. We should pay close attention to the implications, opportunities, and challenges this issue will bring to bear on purchasing power and how it is used.

Minorities Becoming Majorities

Hispanics, Blacks, and Asian Americans, in that order, will ultimately rival whites for majority status in America. One outgrowth of this trend will continue to be more and more interracial marriage and a cross-current of buying and spending patterns not familiar to marketing plans of even the recent past. Ethnic food will continue to gain in popularity—even organized religion may make a comeback. For sure, more products and services will be advertised in Spanish as well as English. It is not inconceivable to me that someday America will have three official languages— English, Spanish, and Chinese.

All companies in all industries will have to take into account in the years ahead the social and consuming differences between the major races in America. The "melting pot" that is our unique heritage will only increase over time to a full boil.

Marketing to the Sexes

Simple in one sense—it's all about hormones. The basic behavioral differences between men and women are influenced by these powerful fluids throughout our lifetimes. And it is just these differences that make *a difference* in successful marketing to the sexes.

Here is a list of behaviors to consider when targeting a product or service to one sex versus another.

- *Impulsiveness.* In general, men tend to shoot from the hip and women are more reasoned in their thinking. But *impulsive* should not be confused with *compulsive.* Women are compulsive shoppers. Men, by and large, are not. Back to the main point—I might wake up one day and decide to go buy a high-end Lexus. My spouse or gal pal isn't wired that way. A woman usually needs to think through the issues before a major purchase. Can I afford to spend the money? What would I be giving up? Can I get a lot of use out of it? Are there good reasons to buy now as opposed to later?

  From an advertising standpoint, this behavioral difference implies that women demand more information than men. Men don't need or generally want a lot of explanation, though they would be better off if they did. Women will actually read the fine print. Most men can't be bothered. A real difference.

- *Practicality.* You can learn a lot by observing men and women in supermarkets. Men want to get in and out as fast as possible. Not their female companions. There are exceptions to every rule, but for the most part women are very sensible when they shop for food—and men are not. Women think value, quality, quantity. Men just don't think! A woman will buy most items at one store and then go to another and another to get a better deal on certain items she felt were too expensive at the first store. In a million years, I would never exhibit that kind of behavior.

- *Allegiance.* Men tend to be more brand loyal than women. Women look for the best deal, the most information, and the practical aspects of a product or service.

Generic products were invented for women, and they buy the majority of them. Quality and top-notch service go a long way with women. Whoever has the highest standards, assuming decent pricing, gets their business. There is, however, a big exception. When it comes to financial services providers, women are more brand loyal. If they have a bad experience or if investment performance is weaker than expected, they are less likely than men to switch from one company to another.

- *Philanthropy.* Americans are a very generous bunch, who collectively give away billions of dollars each year to a variety of charities. Yet it is often the women who stand out. It has been proven time and again that the best prospect for almost all not-for-profit groups is a single, widowed woman over age 60. Still, women of all ages, single, married, divorced, or widowed, have a soft spot for those less fortunate than themselves.

  Men, however, dominate in charitable giving in three categories: colleges, environmental groups, and politicians.

  As alumni, men tend to stay in closer touch with classmates, school news, and particularly with school sports. They prize their alma mater and are interested in its continued stature, and sports success is often 85 percent of their focus. If that were not the case, university coaches wouldn't routinely be making 50 to 100 times more per year than tenured professors.

  Environmental groups find strong support among men who are active in a variety of outdoor sports and recreation. Every year, 12 million men pay for hunting licenses and 50 million for fishing permits. Without abundant, unspoiled land and clear streams and brooks, there would be no hunting and fishing.

  Like the two categories above, contributions to political campaigns are based on practical issues. For the most part, politics heavily affects business, from tax issues to industry legislation. Men still dominate the business landscape and have the strongest desire to support politicians with their wallets, not just their attitudes.

Sports

Without a doubt, men are more sports crazy than women. Sure, there are plenty of women spectators, but how many actually go to a game or watch football on TV if not with a father, brother, son, boyfriend, or spouse? Sports marketing is a huge activity globally and is very male dominated. Sports betting is so big in America, it probably rivals the GNP of many small countries, and interactive betting has just increased the thrill.

Sports team web sites and category sites like the PGA, NFL, and NBA are perfect real estate for advertisers that cater to men. And online ads can be customized to specific games, team members, and times of the day. Even products with no sports tie-in can be successful; for instance, 1–800-Flowers appearing on NBA.com on February 12–14, reminding the guys to not forget their valentines!

Looking Good for Good

Boomers refuse to think or look old. Year after year, attitudinal research highlights that Boomers think they are 10 to 15 years younger than they are. Good news for beauty products! And women spend countless billions on their appearance, from cosmetics and creams to add-on body parts like hair extensions and artificial eyelashes. Plastic surgery is totally mainstream America these days, after hiding out in Hollywood, New York, and Miami for most of the 20th century.

Men are far from immune to vanity's siren call. Men's care products are expanding their lines, and plastic surgery and hair replacement techniques have never been more popular. Many men feel "funny" buying cosmetic-like items at store locations where 98 percent of the traffic is female— though some single men might like the odds! Thus, online works perfectly for millions of men who otherwise would never dream of buying personal care products at a department store.

The old adage still applies: women dress for women and so do men. This difference between the sexes started about 10,000 years ago, so clearly some things never change.

What is changing is that the global population is aging and the beauty/health care category should benefit from increasing demand as far out as our laser readjusted eyes can see.

CHAPTER 19
JINGLES ALL THE WAY

Jingles have become less and less a factor in brand positioning and promotional execution, and that is a mistake—a big mistake.

To understand why jingles can be such a strong marketing force, it's helpful to go back 50,000 years. Initially, music was a way for men and women to choose partners. Later, it became a central part of religious experience. From religion, it morphed into a way to combat fear in battle, and today it is a form of entertainment as well as a powerful medium in which to target consumers with marketing messages.

Beginning with Darwin, many anthropologists agree that music most likely played a key role in mate selection among our ancestors. The basic premise suggests that females, in their search for a good provider of food, clothing, and potential offspring, looked for a male who was so confident of his vigor and position among other males that he had the time to hum a tune, chant, or dance to a rhythmic beat.

Later came religion and, with it, stirring hymns and chants that are an emotional high point for all denominations. Since at least the 10th century, churchgoers have been soothed by music and sing together as an organized expression of their faith. Who can resist the countless Christmas carols and their power to inspire belief in goodwill and cheer to all?

For centuries, armies have marched into battle with drums beating and bands playing. Music can alter mood, and in times of war, it almost acts like a drug to dull the mind to the potential horrors ahead. A similar musical strategy was put to use with the introduction of background music in elevators during the 1920s and 1930s. The fear of being stuck in a small steel box hurtling up and down a newly built skyscraper was assuaged with soothing musical sounds to accompany the ride.

We all know the phrase "silence is golden," and many of us still cherish those quiet, uncluttered moments. But more often, we tune in, log on, plug in, and load more forms of sound than ever before. From the youngest child to the oldest adult, we spend a good part of our day under a musical spell. We wake up to it, listen to it on the way to school or work, and hear it throughout the day in stores and restaurants. In cars, we barely fasten the seat belt before hitting the play button to access state-of-the-art audio systems. And a few years ago, Volkswagen introduced a version of their GTI sedan with an electric guitar hookup. They sold every car in inventory in a matter of weeks.

Although music is often mass-produced, the experience it creates is highly personal. No two people listening to the same melody have exactly the same response. More than ever before, music has become a personal signature, like the selection of a particular ring tone or a popular tune to announce an incoming cell-phone call.

In Japan, imaginative marketers continue to invent new ways to match music with a target audience. Now a Japanese teen can adapt a mobile phone to play background sounds of a party in progress or music in a shopping mall. An enterprising teenage girl can call from her boyfriend's apartment to tell her mom she's still at the mall or her girlfriend's slumber party—not to worry . . . she'll be home first thing in the morning.

What Is a Jingle, and How Is It Used and Misused?

In a very real sense, jingles are commercial hymns. Done well, they are impossible to resist and remain in people's memories from the first few hearings through the rest of their lives.

The dictionary defines a jingle as a memorable advertising slogan set to a catchy melody. To be considered effective, a jingle should literally ring a bell in the brain that immediately registers the product or service the jingle represents.

Despite the power a jingle can wield in consumer purchase decisions, its usage has diminished significantly from the high point of its popularity in the 1950s. The following are several reasons why jingles today are rarely thought about or created:

- Clients no longer demand jingles and rarely ever question why their ad agency never suggests one.
- For the most part, today's marketers have forgotten how powerful sound can be in musical form.
- Few products are marketed with original music and instead rely on popular tunes that don't speak uniquely for the product.
- Marketers who give jingles a try don't give them enough time to become implanted in consumers' minds. If they use jingles at all, they change or drop them after just a few months, driven by the theory that consumers get bored with the same tune over and over again.

It's funny how we often refer to another person as moody or being in a bad mood. Truth be told, we are all "moody" every waking minute of every day. Our brain is hardwired to seek out signals as to how to behave. And the most powerful marker that guides us from mood to mood is music, or in a broader context, sound. It can switch us from one emotion to another with the greatest of ease. While the other senses play their role, they are not as dominant.

The greatest enemy to marketing success is silence. It is particularly true if the advertising effort is restricted to a print medium like newspaper, magazine, or even outdoor. Without the overriding power of music, the ability to evoke any kind of emotion is severely limited.

Make a Jingle Work for You

There is nothing very complicated about a jingle. It's basically an audio brand promise with a clear product or service benefit. It can boost you above your competitors and keep you above them—because a musical signoff on radio or TV or even the Web is hard to ignore and easier to remember than any other ad element.

Many products have been defined by their jingles over the years—from Pepsi to Chock Full o'Nuts (the heavenly coffee) to various beer brands (Schaefer is the one beer to have when you're having more than one) to clothiers, household furnishing establishments, and regional and local businesses numbering in the thousands.

There are plenty of songwriters (beyond Charlie Sheen's character in *Two and a Half Men!*) looking for work who, for a modest fee, can create a unique song that will make your brand come alive and stay alive even long after the jingle is retired.

As proof, the following are *Advertising Age*'s picks for the top 10 jingles over the past 100 years.

Advertising Age Top 10 Jingles of the 20th Century

1. "You deserve a break today" (McDonald's).
2. "Be all you can be" (U.S. Army).
3. "Pepsi Cola hits the spot" (Pepsi).
4. "M'm! M'm! Good" (Campbell Soup).
5. "See the U.S.A. in your Chevrolet" (GM).
6. "I wish I were an Oscar Mayer Wiener" (Oscar Mayer).
7. "Double your pleasure, double your fun" (Wrigley's Doublemint Gum).

8. "Winston tastes good like a cigarette should" (Winston).
9. "It's the real thing" (CocaCola).
10. "A little dab'll do ya" (Brylcreem).

Can a Well-Known Song Define a Product?

Since the late 1980s, popular and mainstream music has been the overwhelming choice for songs that sell products. By the year 2000, original music, commissioned to sell a company or its wares, had become the rare exception to the rule. The benefit of the use of popular music is the instant recall among millions who have enjoyed the tune. The downside is that these songs are not specifically tied to any one brand. For example, while in the kitchen on a quick snack break from your favorite television show, you hear a great pop song coming from your flat screen. Entertaining, but without direct vision, you don't have a clue about what's being sold. My advice is: avoid popular tunes. They can be expensive to secure the commercial rights, and they do not distinguish your product or service—they override it.

A New Term for Spoken Taglines

A jingle is generally defined as a catchy tune that elicits instant recall of a product and, in many cases, its core or most distinctive benefit. I have created an additional term: *tingles*. The dictionary describes tingle as a pinched nerve, and perhaps that's just the right thought. To me, a tingle is a tagline that also serves as a jingle and is sometimes sung and other times spoken with great emphasis in a way that makes it memorable.

The John Houseman campaign for Smith Barney in the mid-1980s is one example. This campaign consisted of 10 television commercials. There was no other media used, so that Houseman's signoff was delivered in only one way. The line was: "Smith Barney. They make money the old-fashioned way . . . they EARNNN it." His unique delivery of the word *earn* was a tingle. It hit you in just the right way, so you would never forget Smith Barney and its association with earning your business.

Karl Malden did a similar job for American Express Travelers Checks with his full, earnest delivery of the line: "American Express Travelers Cheques. Don't leave home without them."

Other examples are: the State Farm tagline, "Like a good neighbor, State Farm is there"; GE's tagline for more than 25 years, "GE. We bring good things to life"; Marlboro cigarettes' "Come to where the flavor is. Come to Marlboro country"; "Pizza Pizza" for Little Caesars; and "Zoom, zoom, zoom" for Mazda.

The combination of a tagline with a forceful and unique spoken or sung cadence is a concrete way to avoid the popular song trap: easy and enjoyable memory of the tune but no recall of your product.

We Have Lost Our Way

Among states and countries competing for tourist dollars, there are only a few examples of tingles. You would think in this multibillion-dollar global battle for visitors, jingles and tingles would be a common way to get attention. And, you would be wrong. There is only one American state that sets its tagline to music, and that's New York State's "I Love New York."

Among countries, you have to go back to the 1980s and a campaign for Spain where the tingle was a five-second singing of the word *Spain* at the end of each radio and television spot.

Today, practically every industry, from financial to drug to auto and packaged goods, has taglines that are rarely if ever spoken, and when they are, more often than not, have no attitude or unique flair. On the Web, company taglines, for the most part, don't appear at all.

If nothing else, we have failed to remember how our minds are wired to seek out and retain interesting delivery of a commercial message in musical or lyrical form. In their effort to make an impact, advertisers have left the distinctive jingle and tingle behind and settled for the low-risk, low-return approach.

We *have* lost our way. We have forgotten what works. We have canceled out millions of years of evolution and billions of promotional dollars by failing to focus on the power of sound—unique sound—in the selling process. Businesses of all sizes need to think more carefully about the opportunity they are missing and start to use the unsung hero of the past: the product-specific jingle or tingle.

CHAPTER 20

THE FUTURE OF MARKETING

Let's start with the obvious. Social networking and all things mobile will continue to connect everyone to friends and family and their popular brands for as far out in the future as we can see—after all, *Star Trek* popularized the handheld mobile device that Americans alive in the 1960s thought then was pure science fiction. Mobile marketing will be a battleground for marketers as they attempt to make sure their apps are front and center versus their competitors. All well and good, but let's review other categories and predict what is to come.

MPP Will Make Customer Service Phone Operators Unnecessary

Back in the late 1980s and through the 1990s, MPP (massive parallel processing) was the state-of-the-art supercomputing solution that many firms employed to cost-effectively store and analyze billions of bytes of customer data. MPP started out as a Defense Department–funded project to speed up the development of stealth technology. This computing method then jumped to oil companies for use in predicting where oil deposits might be. And, eventually, a few consumer-facing firms embraced MPP—most notably Dow Jones and American Express.

The concept for MPP is simple. Prior to its arrival on the scene, all processing was done in serial fashion. Let's say your customer database has 500,000 customer addresses. Using serial processing, when you have a few address changes to enter, the processor literally looks at each customer record in sequence to see if that is the record that matches the address change. It could be the third record or the 3,000th or the 300,000th. In a very large database, this approach can take a lot of processing time. MPP changed this approach by way of mainframes being constructed with multiple processors working in parallel—exactly the way our brains process, albeit with far fewer processors than those in your head. The net effect was that processing speed increased dramatically and allowed marketers to store massive amounts of data and analyze it all instantly instead of in days and weeks using serial processing.

American Express was a prime example. I was responsible in 1991 for putting the American Express cardmember database on an MPP platform—the first-ever use of a supercomputer managing a marketing database. The most amazing change was that what had been a weekly update process, taking a very large IBM traditional mainframe 168 hours a week to complete, with MPP went to 15 minutes. Yes, that's not a typo. Also, ad hoc query against millions of records and billions of bytes of information was available in fractions of seconds versus minutes or hours or even days under the serial method.

In the late 1990s MPP fell out of favor and distributed processing was all the rage. The hardware was cheaper, and many debated whether lightning-fast processing was all that necessary.

But lo and behold, MPP came back with a roar in 2011, when IBM introduced a system called Watson (named after IBM's founder), which was created for the sole purpose of playing *Jeopardy* against human champions of this popular and long-running TV quiz show. Watson has 19 large computers strung together with thousands of processors running in tandem. It is able to listen, speak, answer, and even wager on the Daily Double in fractions of a second—faster than its human competitors. In a series of three games, it trounced the human contestants who were the best of the best over 10 years of the show's previous winners.

Some media commentators have likened Watson to the fictitious HAL computer in the movie *2001: A Space Odyssey*. HAL runs the entire spaceship and decides the crew is a distraction and gets rid of them—except for one!

"So what?" you ask. The "what" is that MPP will enable companies to offer round-the-clock customer service with a computer program answering the phone. And not only answering, but in natural language and responding to a customer's query instantaneously and in a way whereby the customer will think he is speaking to and interacting with a live person. The computer program will even be able to respond to the customer's mood and play off it and show empathy—heretofore thought not possible through computer programming. Oh, and if the customer switches to Spanish or Chinese or any known language, the computer will seamlessly reply in that language. The Gardner Consulting Group, which focuses on marketing applications of technology, predicts the above outcome by the end of this decade—at the latest.

What other marketing/customer service outcomes might MPP help to birth? Clearly, Web interaction will be addressed, for instance, in the form of a personal guide who welcomes you on screen when you visit a company's web site. Some companies attempt this now with merely a figure popping up who has preset answers to certain frequently asked questions. A few years from now, that figure will speak back and forth with you like any human would and with any product or service answer you can think up a question for.

Scary? For some. But exciting, too.

Does PR Have a Role in a World of Instant Communication?

Veteran marketers have been debating for decades the effectiveness of advertising versus public relations (PR). It is a silly argument—like trying to prove that cancer prevention is better than a cancer cure. You need both to control cancer because they complement each other and need each other. The same is true for advertising and PR.

However, for PR to be effective today, it has to play into a news-drenched world with consumer attention spans that are the shortest in human history and will, if anything, keep shortening. The era of sending out a press release and expecting it to become news that is highlighted by major media outlets the next day is dead and buried. With social networking around the clock, anything you are planning to announce usually is already being discussed if it has any value at all. And, often, that discussion isn't what you intended or wished for.

The fundamental issue facing PR today is that it is largely a reactive activity and not proactive. Social networking means you are usually playing catch-up to customer chatter—good, bad, and indifferent.

If for some reason your product, service, or company experiences a negative consumer event, that "news item" will launch through the Web at lightning speed, leaving you little time to respond. And then the question is whether you respond at all or let it blow over and burn itself out. There is no definitive answer to responding to negative publicity, and there never has been, but there are several considerations that can lead to a course of action.

So consider:

- When you get wind of negative opinion circulating about your company, if it has little foundation in truth, you should highlight an official response on your web site and encourage employees and friends to communicate it to their circle of interactive pals.

- Sometimes, unfortunately, major calamities strike that can threaten the very existence of your brand. If that happens, you need a 24/7 crisis command team set up to alert employees and customers, as well as trade press and associated web sites. Your crisis command team should always be on standby and be an integral part of your overall marketing plan. They should practice dry runs and try to plan for the worst possible event or series of events that could strike at any time.

What else should PR focus on today?

Your employees. And you. First, about your employees: you need to take internal communications seriously and put money and time into this activity. At a minimum, make internal PR the sole activity of a single staff person; in a small company, this job can be shared.

No company is successful without highly motivated and knowledgeable employees. For years, psychologists have said the top three issues most important to employees are:

1. Recognition.
2. Treatment as an insider.
3. Appropriate compensation.

Note that money is third on the list.

You need to communicate with your employees all the time. *Always* give them a heads-up on the launch of a new marketing campaign. *Always* ask for their feedback. *Always* alert them to stories about to appear in the press, both positive and negative. *Always* communicate with them as equals. Senior executives must be able and willing to meet with employees regularly and talk frankly about the state of the business.

This leads to another important point: whatever your major business thrust is, you should repeat it and repeat it and keep at it, so employees understand that you are serious about it and they should be as well.

A terrific technique to keep employees up to date is to list a weekly metrics dashboard for your current fiscal year on your intranet site that shows progress to date on your five most important indicators of business success. The only caution here is that you must assume whatever you display will be forwarded by someone to the press, to competitors, and to others who may have a grudge or harbor some ill will.

You

Today, more than ever, every company needs a visible and effective spokesperson to be the "face of the place." Hired spokespeople can be effective as I discussed in an earlier chapter, but they can't be everywhere and do everything, and they can't fill in for you at investor conferences or other events that require a company official.

You or someone in senior management must be accessible to the press and be comfortable and effective in telling your company story as often as required and often with little notice. Whomever you select for this role will need professional coaching and media training to become an effective advocate of your firm. There are a few "naturals" out there, but they are the exceptions. In my 40 years in this business, I have run across only a handful.

Always make sure a PR professional is present when a reporter talks to an employee of any rank, on the telephone or in person. This third-party presence is your protection that what was said becomes what is reported.

Treat reporters with respect and dignity. Remember that 99 percent of the time they make a lot less than you, and whether they admit it or not—they resent it. Never act arrogant or too busy to take time for an interview, assuming they represent a legitimate news outlet. In fact, you should thank them for spending their valuable time with you.

I remember not one but two friends of mine who were CEOs of Fortune 50 companies. Both had interviews a number of years ago with the same major media outlet, and both were panned, along with their companies, in the article that followed their interview. Amazingly, both committed the same three "deadly sins."

1. They both kept the reporters waiting for over an hour.
2. They both commented that they had more pressing matters and couldn't spend much time in the interview.
3. They both said they thought reporters never reported anything accurately.

This story shows that really smart leaders can do really dumb things when representing their company. And where were the PR professionals who should have coached these CEOs long ago about how to win reporters over? It's a mystery to me.

Relationships with the media need to be cultivated and managed in the best interests of the company. This is not manipulation in any way, just basic good manners.

Tips on Interacting with Reporters

Generally, they are a smart bunch, well versed on their subject of expertise but not necessarily well rounded. With a few exceptions, they feel underpaid and underappreciated and apt to lose their job at any minute. And like most people who work on deadlines, they will cut corners to get a story submitted on time.

Here are the basic ways to interact with them:

- Always call back or e-mail back promptly, even if you can't help them.
- Try to give exclusive coverage to two or three key industry reporters on a rotating basis.
- Always be on time for interviews.
- Always request the ability to check facts before a story goes to print.

- If there is a point you really want to make, repeat it several times during an interview—in fact, keep repeating it until you are sick of saying it.
- If you are told you are "off the record," don't believe it. You aren't.
- Buy them a meal occasionally and thank them for covering your business.

What About Investor Relations?

Companies don't do enough to excite and delight shareholders—mostly, it's the reverse. They bore them to death or ignore them completely. You can improve your image by providing regular access to senior executives via conference calls and Web content. Ask for shareholder opinion—all the time. On your web site. In your annual report. Think about setting up a special inbound automated phone number exclusively for shareholder use. These folks will always tell it like it is—good, bad, whatever. Every once in a while, you may even get a *really* good idea.

And don't forget to acknowledge comments promptly. While you are at it, why not have a special product or service offer available only to shareholders. If companies spent more time making shareholders feel special, they might discover a significant source of additional business. Think shareholder marketing instead of shareholder relations. You may not be blood relations, but you do share an interest in the growth of a successful business.

Do Sponsorships Make Sense Anymore— Did They Ever?

No and yes.

You may not like this answer, but, by and large, sponsorships now and in the future are a waste of time and money—especially money. There are two reasons. First, sponsorship opportunities have become outrageously expensive and defy rational allocation of resources. For example, even if Citibank hadn't suffered a near death experience during the Great Recession financial meltdown, agreeing to the naming rights for the New York Mets' new stadium several years ago at $20 million a year for 20 years is just plain absurd. For $1 million or even $2 or $3 million, maybe. And even at that price, it would be a close call.

The second reason for forgoing a sponsorship opportunity is that sponsorships today are so prevalent for every conceivable venue and event that they have lost their ability to help burnish a brand. More likely in this new decade, a company will fall under criticism for throwing bags of money in the lap of a promoter of a sponsorship.

Consumers now more than ever are bombarded with sponsorships at every turn. And speaking of turns, NASCAR plasters corporate logos on every inch of every car and driver—the normal eye can't even sort it all out.

Another trend working against sponsorships is the ever-increasing cost to the consumer of attending a sporting event live with family members in tow. Sports venues are pricing Middle America out of attending pretty much everything except soccer matches. A recent study I saw contends that a family of four is faced with a $500 to $700 tab for attending a Major League Baseball or football game—even during preseason. And we aren't talking super-premium seats. There is a backlash brewing that will generate ill will toward the teams and the companies that sponsor them.

So two streams of advice: If you still want to sponor a venue or event, read the chapter in my first book devoted to sponsorships. What I recommend, though, is to pick a charity that is in a category you can be passionate about and sponsor it with as much visibility as possible and for a very long period of time—like the *New York Times* has done with the Fresh Air Fund for over a century. The Fresh Air Fund is a well-known New York area nonprofit dedicated to sending inner-city kids to summer camp at no cost to their families.

Sponsorships did make sense once upon a time when there were far fewer to be had. And sponsoring charities still does if you sign up as the exclusive sponsor or at least the major one they associate with. If you run a medium to small business, look to local opportunities—Little League, the Boy Scouts, a swim club, that sort of thing.

Popular local, regional, or national radio and TV shows are also possible ways to be associated with content of value that consumers appreciate tuning in to. This course of action assumes you will be the exclusive sponsor and that you will not overpromote during the course of the show. A company that does just the right balance of advertising to show content is BMW for the *Mad Men* series. The next season will air in the summer of 2012. You should check it out.

CHAPTER 21

HOW TO BE A MARKETING STAR

Marketing anything takes a personal commitment to being the number one pitch person much like an effective preacher or political leader who, through the force of his personality, gets folks energized and on board with his prescription for life and the issues that make life rewarding.

Accordingly, you cannot be an effective marketer without being an interesting and entertaining speaker. You need to sway everyone your way—employees, bosses, boards, customers, and anyone and everyone who might happen to hear you at an event or on a podcast or webinar.

If you dread public speaking like most do, get over it. You have to have the ability and the confidence to make your case forcefully to groups that range from 2 to 20 to 2,000, and sometimes more.

You have a large task and not an easy one. You must be able to convince the powers that be in your company that a percentage of your company's hard-earned revenue should be diverted to marketing programs, often with no immediate payback. What your listeners buy, in essence, is *you*. They buy your ability to make things happen. All the great marketing ideas in the world don't mean squat if you can't articulate them, usually with little advance notice, to everyone from your assistant to the CEO.

Suffice to say the number one reason marketers fail is their inability to stand up and get a crowd excited about the mission, the product, and the desired outcome. If you are not an effective speaker, you will fail or at least not be nearly as successful as you could be for you and your company.

I have 10 tips, and the first two are the most important.

1. *Know your material cold.* Seems obvious, but many folks think they do when they do not. The only way to be sure of your subject matter is to keep a few bullet points on a piece of paper you carry around and refer to them constantly—over and over for weeks on end. Eventually, like a stage actor, you will have it all down—cold.

2. *PowerPoint was created to make you appear idiotic.* Oh, and boring beyond belief as well. Everybody, with a few exceptions, uses PowerPoint incorrectly. Humans may be the most brilliant species in the universe, but we cannot listen and look at the same time at a slide full of words and arrows going every which way. Always remember that the main attraction is you, not a bunch of overly crowded slides that are impossible to read or comprehend or remember. If you must use PowerPoint, put one word on a slide and speak to what it means. Or a couple of numbers. Or a compelling visual of the product. That's it. And that's more than enough.

3. *Public speaking is a sport, and you can win the game every time.* There are virtually no naturally gifted public speakers. Think of speaking as a sport that you want to excel at. That means practice, practice, and more practice. Practice any upcoming talk 100 times before you give it. Maybe 200! Also, you have to give as many speeches as you can. Most people are nervous because they rarely speak in public. And they avoid doing so whenever possible. The right approach is just the opposite. Public speaking must become second nature to you. And that will happen only if you get

up on your feet as often as the opportunity presents
itself.

4. *Unless you are president of the United States, never read a
speech word for word.* A better approach is use 3″ × 5″
cards bulleted with the major points you want to
cover. Do not be afraid to hold these cards in your
hands. You can walk around a stage with them—even
throw them on the floor one by one as you proceed
through your talk like David Letterman does with his
Top Ten cards—he throws them out an imaginary
window! It is good to show some flair and not take
yourself too seriously.

5. *Podiums were invented to make you look like a stiff.*
Sometimes a room is set up so that you must use a
podium when no other sound equipment is available except on it. Fine. But otherwise, you should
be miked on your body and stand with no barrier
between you and your audience. Even better, walk
within and around the seated audience—it makes you
one of them and is intimate and engaging.

6. *When in doubt, cut out.* Whatever amount of time you
are given to speak at a public event, have a talk that
takes half that time. Not to worry—you will carry on
longer than you think. Also remember to pause frequently from one major point to the next. And repeat
a point for added emphasis.

7. *A trick with video clips.* No one teaches you this in those
high-priced MBA programs: when showing video clips,
insert seven-second spacing to give your audience time
to absorb one clip and get ready to watch the next.
This spacing also allows you to set up the next clip with
a few words to alert your audience to what's next.

8. *Always have high energy.* Speaking is acting, plain and
simple. You need to be up and energetic throughout your entire presentation. That energy will spread
among your audience. Notice how certain politicians
(think: Bill Clinton) or very compelling preachers
(Al Sharpton) can fire up a group. A lot has much more

to do with the speaker's high energy level than the actual material.

9. *The fewer points, the better.* Never have a long laundry list of points, as in "I will be discussing the following 10 points over the next hour." Your audience will immediately hope the ceiling caves in and ends their misery. Stick with smaller numbers, as in "I will cover four major reasons why we must change the way we do business around the globe."

10. *Last but not least, don't be Adam or Eve.* Remember, they were fine running around Eden naked until they ate the wrong apple and discovered they had "privates." And so, ever since, when standing in front of an audience, the prevailing pose is hands over these same privates—otherwise known as the fig leaf pose. Even seasoned politicians and TV commentators, who should know better, often don't. *Avoid* this gesture at all times. It is a weak and lame pose and makes anyone, even George Clooney or Angelina Jolie, look pathetic—and that's hard to do! I don't care where you put your hands—in the air, in your pockets, behind you . . . just not covering your reproductive organs.

Franklin Roosevelt was once asked about guidelines for making presentations. He said there are three basic rules:

1. Walk to the podium and smile.
2. Get to the point.
3. Sit down.

So be it.

Managing Your Staff

Far too many marketing professionals and their bosses and the human resource "experts" measure success by the number of direct reports they have, the total head count in the marketing department, and the size of the marketing budget. This supposed measure of one's marketing ability is nonsense. To be a real marketing star you have to know how to inspire and manage people. You have to come up with ideas that they can embrace and that will significantly move the business needle. You don't need large numbers of direct reports to bog down the time you have to think about moving your business forward. You need to stay focused on outfoxing the competition and on exciting and delighting customers and potential customers. Period.

You need to come up with big ideas that will work in the marketplace. You need to have an endless stream of ideas and be able to sort out which are just plain undoable and which could possibly be in the breakthrough category.

And most ideas will fail immediately after "birth," which is why you need a lot of them. Even the greatest marketer on the planet today—Steve Jobs—has had some spectacular failures, including a PC called Lisa, the Newton, Apple TV, and the first Apple Portable, to name a few. Invention, by its very nature, is a series of mistakes or seemingly wrong paths taken that ultimately lead to a positive outcome. Why should marketing be any different?

If you don't want to think and experiment and tinker and doodle and think some more about how to get customers to love you and buy more, you may still deserve to be some-where on the marketing team, but you will never be the star.

You also need to provide a work environment that encourages free thinking and fresh initiative. And you have to report to someone who understands this point. There are three questions that require a "yes" answer for you to be a star with your company and your team:

1. Do you have really good chemistry with your boss and colleagues?
2. Do you have the latitude to do the job of transform-ing the company's marketing from okay to great? After all, why take a job just to do okay marketing?

> ## Avoiding the Failure of a Great Idea
>
> To a very large degree, the success of any marketing effort boils down to one designated individual sweating the details—specifically, the details of watching over all aspects of fulfillment. In plain language, making sure the product or service is delivered in a way that meets or, better yet, exceeds customer expectations. It is not enough to rely on an outside service, especially one that is miles or continents away from your offices like many customer service centers are today.
>
> You need a professional who is accountable to you. It should also be someone who loves the challenge and science of what happens from the time an order is placed to the time you get an acknowledgment of receipt from the customer.
>
> Your fulfillment expert should be highly motivated and highly rewarded for a job well done.

3. Is there a commitment to spend the money if great ideas are forthcoming?

Pretty simple rules of engagement to work by. And absolutely necessary for marketing success.

How to Manage an Ad Agency So You Both Succeed

I am not sure who came up with this line that really says it all: "Clients get the advertising they deserve." For many decades now, most agency relationships have been mismanaged, and the proof is that most advertising is lacking in appeal or any semblance of being memorable or inspirational to the consumer.

Most companies with ad budgets want safe advertising, and that is what they get. But safe doesn't equal the phrase "beat the pants off the competition." Reminds me of ad man Jerry Della Famina's famous quote, "Advertising is the most fun one can have with their clothes on."

Maybe that was true 20 years ago. Today, agencies are micromanaged by clients who make ridiculous accusations of supposed conflicts along with sucking *all* the risk-taking out of the creative process.

To manage an agency properly you need exactly the same two attractions that make couples into happy and loving twosomes—chemistry and trust. In fact, mutual business "love" with your agency team is essential if there is going to be real rapport between your staff and theirs and a true feeling of partnership. If there is no bonding, find another agency team fast.

How do you measure chemistry?

- You like exchanging ideas, concerns, hopes, and dreams with the personnel assigned to you.
- You enjoy occasional socializing with them over drinks or a meal or sporting event, and so on.
- You can completely trust them with confidential information—from the head account person to the summer intern.
- You can tell that the agency is genuinely interested in your business.

Next, always remember an agency's product is its people. It all boils down to the golden rule: treat your agency team as you would expect to be treated—praise good work and pay for it. If you want to nickel and dime your agency, which so many clients seem to find ego satisfaction in doing, don't expect their best thinking and the brightest media planners and creatives on your account.

By all means, give criticism and make it constructive. Your goal is to be the client that personnel throughout the agency want to be assigned to. That requires insisting on teamwork, encouraging big ideas, and joining in brainstorming sessions.

Then there's the money. In most large companies, the finance and procurement people have a large say in how agencies should be compensated. If you run a small firm, then look in the mirror. Either way, being finance driven with an agency doesn't work. It doesn't inspire and doesn't create an environment where out-of-the-box thinking and big ideas flourish. Focusing on beating down agencies on their compensation is partly the reason why there is so little exceptional marketing and advertising done.

What to do about it? We marketers should bring the finance and procurement folks into "our tent" and make them part of the overall agency team on the client side. This way, they will come to understand the value of the creative process and how, if supported properly, the marketing outcomes can transform a business and its bottom line.

The biggest barriers to successful marketing promotion are (1) stifling creative thinking and (2) trying to do a campaign on the cheap. Many clients are guilty of both these actions and yet wonder why they just keep treading water.

Most finance types on the client side never see an agency presentation or ever meet a creative director or media planner. No wonder they are less than thrilled with the bills they see for creative services. It's all extremely undefined for them. Who are these agency people? What makes them worth the money we pay? The solution, as mentioned earlier, is to make the finance/procurement folks part of the core team on the client side. They should attend most of the joint meetings and get involved in the ongoing planning process. Few do this. You should.

As for compensation, agencies seem fixated on charging by the hour. I have no problem with this approach insofar as they need to calculate what they pay each employee per hour. But beyond the pure math, this fixation with billing by the hour makes no "cents."

The creative process never has and never will lend itself to two hours of thinking about marketing solution A and four hours about solution B. Nor does copywriting, or layout and design, or media planning. Creative thinking and inspiration can come at any time: in the middle of the night, over a scotch, during a six-mile jog, even while watching a movie or sitting in a boring meeting—probably anchored by an incomprehensible PowerPoint presentation.

I don't care how many hours a person punches on the clock during the day. I am paying for their brainpower and the use of a team to do a certain project over a specific period of time. Within that time period they should feel free to think about my business at any time, in any situation, without worrying about the exact hours they put in on a certain day, or week, or month. Agencies and clients need to remember that the value of a passionate idea or a new visual approach to the business that pops up one evening while walking the dog can't be quantified by an hourly rate. *Great* work comes out of the freedom of ignoring a daily hours-spent log.

The best approach to agency compensation is to agree to a monthly fee that covers *all* expected work. If the scope of the assignment significantly changes, then either side should be allowed to request a review and the fee should be adjusted accordingly.

What We Take for Granted We Shouldn't— Great Writing

You are probably not a Hollywood insider, but your awareness of good writing has probably been honed by that industry. Oscar-winning movies like *The Godfather* and *Patton* or, more recently, *The King's Speech* and *Social Network* would not be worldwide smash hits without stellar screenplays. TV sitcoms and dramas are no different. From *All in the Family* to *Frasier* and *Friends* and *Two and a Half Men*, the actors are just one-dimensional nobodies without a great script.

Just as in these popular shows, copy is the single most important element in any marketing effort. It is the voice of your product or service and delivers your message. Its impact cannot be underestimated. But just how much is copy worth, and how do you properly motivate and compensate a copywriter?

As mentioned earlier, most ad agencies still bill by the hour, which may make some sense for account management personnel, but no sense for creative activities like copywriting.

How long does it take to write a good promotional letter, or print ad campaign, or TV script for a 30-second commercial? Who knows? Sometimes a day, sometimes a week, sometimes 15 minutes. I have written ads in my head while jogging and on a note pad while waiting for a movie to start. This is common practice among writers, especially in the marketing world.

Given that the creative process follows no logical process, you should pay writers by the project and settle up front on the fee—exactly, by the way, how Hollywood scriptwriters are paid. There are no hard-and-fast rules. Writers are a funny bunch. Some think they are worth a lot, and some are worth way more than they think. Sometimes just one good line is priceless.

Often, the best way to pay an agency, or the writer if he is freelance, is based on a day rate. If the copy gets done in 15 minutes and is brilliant, why should you care how long it took to create?

A day rate for a seasoned copywriter can run from $2,500 to as much as $10,000. Think Moroccan bazaar and negotiate. For unknown reasons, writers have a desire to bargain. Negotiations with writers usually take place in two dimensions: what they think their day rate should be, and how many days they think the project will take. For most small projects, you should pay for a day or two of their time. For a major multimedia campaign, you might consider a flat monthly fee for one to three months.

One "trick" I suggest is that once you agree to a price, you should surprise the writer the next day by offering to add a bit more to the fee. Nothing makes writers feel better than the belief that you spent time thinking their work was worth more than you originally agreed. I know this sounds silly, but it really works. Like creatives in any field, writers are insecure and have a high need for approval. "How did I do?" This thought is always on their minds. Make them feel great and they will work harder to please you and create something really special.

CHAPTER 22

EIGHT TIPS TO BEING MORE CREATIVE

Everybody envies the truly creative personality—think Albert Einstein, Steve Jobs, Steven Spielberg, Carl Sagan, Stanley Kubrick, and so on. And we all wish we could snap our fingers and create something truly memorable that would outlast us and serve as a legacy for all time. Only a tiny percentage of all living souls since the beginning of time have been so blessed, but there are techniques that can make you a creative star beyond what you think may be possible—and have you enjoy the satisfaction of having a decent chance of being the "inventor" of some aspect of break through marketing.

Here are my suggestions to help propel you on that path:

- *When others zig, you should zag.* Avoid conventional wisdom and seek the opposite. Example: All your competitors compete on offering the lowest price. You might say your product costs more and it is worth it. Most consumers will pay more for a truly better outcome. In fact, you might try radically different pricing. For instance, if you offer an annual membership fee, you might try suggesting there is no set fee—the consumer should pay whatever they think annual membership is really worth. The point is to break out of the mold and take risks—test them, sure—but take them.

- *We all have creative moments.* We just need to capture them when they occur. And they can occur at any moment, anywhere. Always carry a blank piece of paper and a pencil or pen to write down an idea when it pops into your head. Even in the bathroom. Okay—you think this approach is too low tech for the digital age? Then never be more than an arm's length from your iPhone or Blackberry. For many folks today, these devices are their "third appendage." Type the idea into the notes section or even send yourself an e-mail or a text message. I do this all the time when a new idea comes literally to mind.

- *Force yourself to do things completely foreign to your common interests.* I occasionally pick up a woman's gossip magazine or an issue of *Scientific American,* where many of the articles baffle me but I give them a thorough read nonetheless. If you are of a liberal bent, read an op-ed by a conservative you thoroughly disagree with. Or the reverse if you are a conservative. Practically no one can be a creative marketer without being well read across a wide range of topics and points of view. So you don't like opera? Go to one anyway. Hate shopping with your spouse? Delight her by saying yes sometimes. You can learn a lot by trailing a mate or significant other through a supermarket or any number of different stores. You can't be creative without experiencing completely different experiences.

- *Think like a customer.* We think we do, but usually we don't. And remember, customers rarely think about your service or product. And when they do, it is usually for a few seconds now and then. Therefore, how can you grab their attention when they have none?

How can you excite and delight them visually or with sound mixed in that literally stops them in their tracks. As I state throughout this book, you need to think about injecting personality and some edginess into your promotional activities. Example: Airlines all sound the same in their pitch to take your bucks and cram you into a small seat in the bargain. But one applies humor and a personal touch to everything it does. Visit Jet Blue's web site and you will see what I mean.

- *Spend a lot of time on competitors' web sites.* And for that matter, on lots of different web sites across a broad spectrum of topics. You will likely get bored to tears, which is the point. This activity will help you direct the reengineering of your web site. If you want to see a really fun and engaging web site, google Bitter Lawyer, which is a site catering to young lawyers who resent being low folk on the slow boat to someday maybe destination partner.

- *Go visit an Apple store.* Completely unlike most other retail outlets. It is swarming with smart sharp sales folk who become your tour guide, salesperson, and cashier all wrapped into one cool experience. Everything about an Apple store is different from the traditional way retail stores operate. Perhaps your business can take similar steps with its retail outlets or when creating an online environment. We live in a rapidly changing modern age that requires more open space, instead of the cramped and crowded feeling most stores and web sites project. Apple leads the way.

- *Think every day of how your business should operate in 5 years and 10 years.* This suggestion may sound pretty basic, but few marketers really do it. We are all just attempting to help make next quarter's numbers. As Alvin Toffler famously said in his best seller, *Future Shock,* "The only thing permanent is change." I also like Mae West's great line when being propositioned in a hotel lobby: "I used to be Snow White, but I drifted." We will drift into the future whether we like it or not. No business can survive today or, more to the point, tomorrow without changing its sales pitch and product mix and customer experience on a regular basis. You need to embrace change all the time and lead the effort when everything seems fine and the troops don't want to change how they sale and service your customers.

- *Sometimes the best advice comes from "the bottom."* Do yourself a favor and go cold turkey on paying high-priced consultants to help you move your business forward. The folks who know the most are your employees in the trenches who face or speak to customers and prospects every day. I am amazed how many supposedly smart C-suite executives and the boards that employ them listen to only consultants exactly like them who have no experience interacting with customers on a daily basis. Very often high-level strategy is so far removed from customer—facing reality that the two never sync up and companies never achieve the success they would if their strategy actually started with regularly polling their own employees—and not on workplace issues, but rather on customer insights gleaned from interacting with customers and prospects every day. Tracking customer satisfaction metrics helps, but it's real employee-customer interaction that has hidden diamonds of opportunity to improve on your existing business platform.

CHAPTER 23

STEAL THESE SECRETS NOW

I t has been fun writing this new edition, and, like the first version, I am ending with 10 "secrets" that shouldn't be. It is a mystery to me why so much marketing money is wasted on lame promotions that don't have to be. The sad truth is that marketing today relies on too many metrics and not enough understanding of the basic techniques of persuasion that have guided human behavior since commerce first began centuries ago. Part of the problem has to do with thinking that being in the digital age means new rules apply. For the most part they do not. The real change is the number of channels or customer touch points that must be considered and addressed. What used to be called integrated marketing is more important today than any time in marketing history.

So steal all of these secrets and set forth on a journey of success for you, your company, and all of the consumers you touch and delight. These secrets are not ranked in order of importance. They are all equally important.

- *What makes consumers tick.* Regardless of age and ethnic background, the three big issues in our lives are keeping healthy, seeking financial security, and enjoying the company of family and close friends. Everything else is secondary. Consumers are also overtaxed with digital and mobile messages and have little spare time, energy, or interest in boring or copy-heavy promotions. With regard to selling anything to anybody, never has there been a better time to execute on the theme "less is more." Show the product in a compelling manner and describe the two or three reasons that it is indispensable.

- *Three essential marketing ingredients.* These never change and are also rarely deployed as well as they should be. Successful marketing campaigns must be visually exciting, highlight a few new features, and include a thoroughly compelling call to action. Working together, these three elements should stop viewers or readers in their tracks, make them pay attention to the message, and get them to act on it quickly. The most common waste of advertising dollars is producing brand advertising, most notably for television, and having a nearly invisible and lame call to action. Do not allow this to happen. Insist that every form of advertising makes it crystal clear that you want to hear from the consumer and that they will be better off for it. Geico does it correctly with their headline "15 minutes could save you 15 percent. Call us at_____."

- *The digital age still requires a unique selling proposition (USP).* Think Apple, FedEx, Whole Foods, Walmart, Geico, the glass Coke bottle, even Las Vegas and Viagra—every successful brand must have a visual or written USP that sets the brand apart from competitors and makes it special. Remember that a brand is a promise that delivers an experience—hopefully, a unique and value-added experience. The USP should be clear, concise, and completely understood by every single employee and every single customer and potential customer as well.

- *Art directors can't see reality.* And their reality is they design ads that no normal human can actually read. That must be why they insist on using white reverse sans serif type 98 percent of the time instead of serif typefaces (type with feet) in primary colors that most print comprehension studies cite as being 10 to 100 times easier to read. I am serious when I say do not allow art directors to do their own thing. Tell them exactly what type to use, and however big they make it, tell them to triple the size.

- *Never change a great tagline (brand promise).* Consumers don't get tired of the same brand promise. They want it to be the same year after year, decade after decade. BMW will never change "the ultimate driving machine," now in use close to 50 years, nor will De Beers change "a diamond is forever," which first came on the scene in 1947. Or consider Marlboro with its request since 1955 to "come to Marlboro country." Thus, three of the most successful brands of all time have never changed their taglines. If you have a great one, insist on keeping it. If you don't, pay a great writer to create one for you.

- *Focus groups are a complete waste of money.* That's not a misprint! They are. Why pay 10 to 40 people who do not live and breathe your business to tell you how to run it? Absurd. If you want to focus folks on your business, ask your employees to give you the skinny on how improvements to your product or service can be made. If you still want consumer advice, use a firm that specializes in online research, which is very cheap and can get responses quickly from thousands of consumers, not a handful.

- *Rethink marketing to e-mail addresses.* On average, companies have only 17 percent of their customers' e-mail addresses. The reason is that consumers are wary that they will be bombarded with e-mail marketing messages if they give their address to the brands they do business with. And most of the time, the consumer is right. The way to convince them otherwise is to (1) make it crystal clear that their e-mail address will not be given out to any other company, and (2) suggest that they create a personal portal at your web site so that you then send them an e-mail only when brand new offers that target their interests are available for their review on their personalized Web page.

- *The power of personality.* It should be totally obvious that people want to hear about an offer from other people and not from a company. Then why do most marketers ignore this fact? They should not—especially when today we are so into social networking, which just reinforces my point. There is nothing more powerful to breaking through the clutter of daily ad bombardment than picking an effective spokesperson who is an integral part of your unique selling proposition. Finding just the right person or animal or animated character is something you should view as critical to your company's success. The world revolves, and always has, around religious leaders, political leaders, and business leaders. The consumer world fixates on characters—Ronald McDonald, the gecko, the Pillsbury Doughboy, to name a few. And consumers will be attracted to real people if they are credible and passionate about the company they represent. The gold standard was John Houseman for Smith Barney, Frank Purdue for Purdue Chicken, and Karl Malden for American Express.

- *10,000 years of social networking and what it means today.* Social networking is a term for what we have always craved—news that we can talk to others about. Technology makes this activity more fun, a million times more robust, and instantaneous on a global basis—from the backyard barbecue in Kansas to a street protest in Iran to who attended our new baby's christening. In a commercial context, every company needs a strategy and a dedicated team to leverage networking sites and do everything from product research to recruiting, to viral sales, to crisis management, and often in real time.

- *Loyalty programs have changed.* Like so much else in the digital era, they are now best in class when they reward consumers in real time. No one has the patience to wait months or years for a reward for repeat purchases. We want instant recognition at every consumer-facing point of sale. This interactive loyalty landscape means you must employ state-of-the-art database management. The good news is that small companies can buy marketing database services for a fraction of what they used to cost and thus compete with the "Big Boys."
- *The most underleveraged piece of data on your customer is how many consecutive years he has been a customer.* The vast majority of companies store this data, yet never use it to remind the customer that they appreciate his patronage year after year after year. Crazy, when you consider that consumers are ticked pink, and every other color, when companies make an effort to thank them for consecutive-year loyalty. And there is virtually no extra cost in highlighting this recognition point when customers log in or call you or receive a mailing from you. Fundamental fact: the more years of consecutive association, the more profitable the customer—especially if you remind him that you are aware of and appreciate his ongoing loyalty.
- *Speak up.* You cannot be a marketing star without being a star speaker. There are probably three natural-born speakers on the planet—and you aren't one of them. So grab the microphone and spend some bucks to hire a speaking coach for a few sessions. How many? A good coach will tell you when you are ready to go solo. You will never regret spending the time and money to become a speaker who can excite and entertain an audience. And regularly reread my tips on how to be an effective speaker—until you are.
- *There are six reasons to advertise.* And they are the same I highlighted in my first book. In order of importance:

1. Motivate your employees and make them feel proud of how you portray their hard work.
2. Remind existing customers why they continue to be.
3. Generate new leads.
4. Recruit great people from your competitors.
5. Get noticed by the press and gain more awareness from the public in doing so.
6. Build the brand. More awareness is always good. But don't forget to ask for the order.

ABOUT THE AUTHOR

Steve Cone is executive vice president of AARP, one of the world's largest membership organizations, which numbers over 36 million Americans. Previously, Steve served as chief marketing officer of Epsilon from 2007 to early 2010.

Steve is one of the most respected figures in marketing today. Over his 40-year career he was a key figure in creating many of the airline, hotel, and retail loyalty programs millions participate in as well as major campaigns for Apple, American Express, Federal Express, and other global brands.

Steve has also been tapped for advice by presidential candidates from both parties and was instrumental in raising the funds to build the Vietnam Memorial in Washington, D.C.

INDEX